N & N

Global Studies

Ten Day Review

Authors:

John Osborne
North Salem High School
North Salem, New York

Sue Ann Kime
Arlington High School
LaGrangeville, New York

Regina O'Donnell
New York Archdiocesan Schools
Cardinal Spellman High School, Bronx, NY

Editors:

Wayne Garnsey and Paul Stich
Wappingers Central Schools
Wappingers Falls, New York

Cover Design, Illustrations, and Artwork:

Eugene B. Fairbanks
John Jay High School
Hopewell Junction, New York

N & N Publishing Company, Inc.
18 Montgomery Street   Middletown, New York 10940
(914) 342 - 1677

Dedicated to our students, with the sincere hope that

Global Studies — Ten Day Review

will further enhance their education and better prepare them
with an appreciation and understanding of the people
and historical events that have shaped our world.

Special Credits

Thanks to the many teachers who have contributed their knowledge, skills,
and years of experience to the making of our 10 Day Review.

To these educators, our sincere thanks
for their assistance in the preparation of this manuscript:

Cindy Fairbanks
Anne McCabe
Virginia Page
William Schlink
Victor Salamone
Gloria Tonkinson

Special thanks to our understanding families.

Global Studies — Ten Day Review has been produced on the
Macintosh II and LaserMax 1000.
  MacWrite II by Claris and *Canvas* by Deneba were used to produce
text, graphics, and illustrations. Original line drawings were repro-
duced with *VersaScan* on a Microtek MSF-300ZS scanner and modi-
fied with *DeskPaint* by Zedcor. The format, special designs, graphic
incorporation, and page layout were accomplished with *Ready set Go!*
by Manhattan Graphics.
  Special technical assistance was provided by Frank Valenza and
Len Genesee of *Computer Productions*, Newburgh, New York.
  *To all, thank you for your excellent software, hardware, and techni-
cal support.*

Printed in the United States of America

SAN # 216-4221   **ISBN # 0935487-48-4**
3 4 5 6 7 8 9 0 BM 0 9 8 7 6 5 4 3

Table of Contents

To the Student

The authors of this book are all experienced social studies teachers. We have designed this book to share with you our ideas on preparing for the Examination in Global Studies.

We have found that students consistently lose more points on the Part II written response questions than they do on the Part I multiple choice questions. We believe the reason for this is that students misunderstand the requirements of these questions, leave sections out, or fail to furnish factual data to substantiate their opinions.

To help you overcome these problems, the nine sections of this book focus on the concepts and issues on which exam questions are most frequently based.

The questions based on these global issues and concepts cross time periods covered in the Global Studies course. You are usually asked to illustrate your knowledge of these common ideas by choosing from a series of examples. In fact, the sheer number of choices to be made is often confusing to many students.

To help you approach the exam in an organized way, each of the 9theme segments of the book have the same structure: background readings, related graphic materials, theme-based multiple choice questions, and a model essay.

The **Model Essay** is the core exercise. It is a unique pre-writing technique which has been successful with our own students. There are three goals that can be achieved by using the pre-writing grid exercise:

- First, you will be able to see all the parts of the question needed to earn full credit.
- Second, it requires you to write down the proper amount of relevant factual data.
- Third, it provides an outline from which the final version of your answer can be constructed.

To help you prepare the essays, review the **Glossary of Topically Related Terms** on pages 112 through 128. The terms are organized according to specific topics and include many more individuals, events, places, and concepts than are found in the 9 lessons.

Training yourself with this exercise should help you analyze questions and write clear and concise answers. At the same time, you will be reviewing the major ideas of the course. We wish you great success on the examination.

The Authors

Assignments

Lesson	Issues	Pages	Questions	Date Due
1				
2				
3				
4				
5				
6				
7				
8				
9				
10				

LESSON 1

War and Peace

Wars have been fought for centuries for diverse reasons. In the Middle Ages as well as during modern times, one of the key issues has always been **power**. During the Renaissance and Reformation, as well as in the current Middle East disputes, **religion** was and is still an important cause of wars. *Why* **Imperialism**, **nationalism**, **militarism**, and **ideology** have been major causes of wars during the 19th and 20th Centuries.

There have also been many changes in methods of warfare. The armor, the crossbow, and the long bow of the Middle Ages gave way to gunpowder and the cannon. The technology of the 19th and 20th Centuries has given us sub- *How* marines, aircraft, poison gas, atomic and hydrogen bombs, and missile delivery systems. Also, the 20th Century has seen the rise of **terrorism** (systematic use of violence to force a group to do something).

Wars are obviously destructive in terms of lives and property, but there is also some evidence that wars can be *Result* vehicles of **cultural diffusion**. The campaigns of Alexander the Great, the Roman imperial conquests, the Crusades, the Hundred Years War, and the Napoleonic Wars, as well as the world wars of the 20th Century have caused interactions of people which have led to new cultural and economic patterns of existence.

The peace settlements which follow wars have tremendous impact on subsequent history. In some cases, they *Result* have been causes of later wars. Agreements forged at the **Congress of Vienna** (1814-1815) and the **Paris Peace Conference** (Versailles, 1919) established international organizations designed to preserve peace. At the same time these treaties contained arrangements which set the scene for future wars.

World Issue   1

War and Peace in the Napoleonic Era

Napoleon Bonaparte's 1799 coup d'etat in France was made possible partially because of his reputation as a military hero. Napoleon seemed to promise glory, as well as stability, after ten years of revolutionary disorder.

At first, Napoleon was successful against the enemies of France. He continued the use of the citizen army and used his leadership ability to inspire his soldiers to undertake forced marches. His amassed artillery and strategic use of reserves, along with the inability of his enemies to unite, were important factors in his success.

At the peak of Napoleon's power, France controlled or was allied with almost all countries on the European continent. Napoleon's ultimate defeat can be explained in terms of the difficulty of controlling a large empire, the power of the British Navy, the Russian winter and its "scorched earth policy," and the resistance of the Spanish.

Napoleon Bonaparte

The **Congress of Vienna** met after Napoleon's last defeat to redraw the boundaries of Europe and restore Europe's 18th Century political structure. It had only limited success. It ignored the forces of nationalism and revolutionary idealism which Napoleon's armies had spread across Europe. As a consequence, Spanish, Italian, Belgian, Polish, and other peoples revolted to gain independence or a voice in their governments.

An international organization known as the **Concert of Europe** was supposed to preserve the Congress of Vienna settlement and prevent a resurgence of French power. Initially, it was somewhat successful.

Later, however, the British and a new liberal French government refused to help the Concert put down revolutions in other countries when their national interests were not directly involved. Nevertheless, there was not another general European war until World War I (1914-1918).

World War II

World War II (1939-1945) had numerous causes: the **Paris Peace Conference** which settled World War I (Treaty of Versailles), the economic stress resulting from the Great Depression, the power and expansionist goals of the fascist dictatorships, and the weak appeasement policies of the democracies.

After World War I, many Germans felt that the makers of the Treaty of Versailles had been grossly unfair to them. They resented the reparations, limits on their military capacity, loss of their colonies, and especially the humiliation of the war guilt clause.

In the 1930's, **Adolf Hitler** and the leaders of the **Nazi Party** were able to use this resentment to win popular support for their radically nationalistic program. Through the use of an intensive propaganda program, the Nazis promised Germans that they would overturn the treaty and build up the German military to restore national glory. The Nazi goal was **lebensraum** (living space). It translated into German expansion into Eastern Europe.

Adolf Hitler

Similar imperialist desires were evident in both Italy and Japan. The Italians under **Mussolini** wanted "**mare nostrum**" (control of the area around the Mediterranean), and the Japanese wanted to control a vast empire in East Asia.

In the 1930's the Axis nations launched a series of aggressive military actions in Manchuria, Ethiopia, and Austria. The Western European democracies were weak because of the Great Depression. They followed a pattern of diplomatic **appeasement**. To avoid a general war, the Western European nations gave the aggressor Axis nations what they wanted.

During World War II, human rights were seriously violated by Hitler's attempted genocide of the Jews and Stalin's massacres of people in Ukraine and Poland and other border areas of the Soviet Union. Technological development during the war led to synthetics, crude missiles, radar, and the atomic bomb first used by the U.S. against the Japanese city of Hiroshima.

Also during the war, a series of Allied conferences (Casablanca, Cairo, Tehran, Yalta) laid the basis for the peace. The scene was created for Europe to become divided between the communist East and the democratic nations of the West. The **United Nations** was established to preserve the peace by eliminating the underlying causes of war and providing a format for discussion of problems by nations.

The Cold War

The **Cold War**, which followed World War II, was fought by all methods short of all out war between the **superpowers**. The democracies established the **NATO** alliance in Western Europe, and the Soviets countered with the **Warsaw Pact** in Eastern Europe. The U.S. followed a policy of **containment** (prevent the expansion of communism), and the U.S.S.R. sought to build a series of protective puppet states along its borders.

In the midst of the evolving Cold War tensions, the **Korean War** broke out. Communist North Korea invaded South Korea in June, 1950. A U.N. Army was created and placed under American leadership while the communist nations aided North Korea. In 1953, a truce reestablished the border between the two Koreas, approximately where it was before the war began.

Cold War tension also led to U.S. involvement in the Vietnam War. After France withdrew from its former colony in 1954, North Vietnam invaded the South. The guerrilla tactics of the North Vietnamese were very costly. Also, there was considerable domestic opposition to the war effort in the United States. A cease-fire agreement which led to American withdrawal was signed in 1973. The North Vietnamese quickly took over the South and unified the country under a communist government.

The roles of the superpowers in the Middle East can also be regarded as part of the Cold War. The United States became a defender of Israel's democracy, while the Soviets aided Israel's hostile Arab neighbors. As with the U.S. in Vietnam, the Soviet involvement in Afghanistan proved costly and controversial. After a decade of frustration against anti-communist guerrilla forces, Soviet President Gorbachev ordered a withdrawal.

The Cold War struggles subsided in the 1990's. Significant changes in Eastern Europe, Western Europe, and the United States ended the power struggles. Communist regimes lost power in most of the areas of Eastern Europe and the newly independent republics of the former U.S.S.R. Apparently, the era of intense competition between totalitarian communism and democratic capitalist systems closed. However, intense ethnic and nationalistic differences remain. Croatia, Bosnia, Slavenia, and Macedonia have broken away from Yugoslavia. The Serbs and Croats engaged in bitter fighting. In former Soviet Union Republics there is fear of civil war and starvation. The Communist Party has lost power but is still an active force in the politics of the region. Political unrest will remain a problem in this region for a long time.

Terrorism

what

Terrorism is used by small, desperate groups wishing to call world attention to grievances and objectives. Terrorists represent different nationalist, ethnic, religious, and ideological causes. They employ kidnapping, hijacking, suicidal raids, bombings, and assassinations. Because they lack the military and political power of nations, they justify such violence as "warfare" to gain their objectives. The fear generated by a series of wanton attacks against innocent people is considered a weapon in itself.

Responses to terrorism vary. Some nations and people wage counterstrikes or execute the terrorists they have captured previously. Others resist violent responses but increase security at airports and other likely targets.

The war which created Israel in 1948 displaced the Arab inhabitants of Palestine. Refugee camps became "home" to over a million Arabs of the region awaiting a settlement on their homeland. The **Palestinian Liberation Organization (PLO)** emerged in the refugee camps in the 1960's. The group, headed by **Yassir Arafat**, is dedicated to reestablishing a sovereign Palestinian nation on the west bank of the Jordan River and control of the holy city of Jerusalem.

Extremist groups affiliated with the PLO have been responsible for numerous terrorist acts, including, killing Israeli athletes at the 1972 Munich Olympics, hijacking and killing tourists on the Mediterranean cruise ship Achille Lauro in 1985.

Groups within the **Islamic Shi'ite fundamentalist movement** have also practiced terrorism. Leaders in Iran, Syria, Lebanon, and Libya have allowed Shi'ite groups to use their countries as terrorist bases.

After Shah Mohammed Reza Pahlavi was forced to abdicate the throne of Iran in 1979, Shi'ite leader **Ayatollah Ruhollah Khomeini** established an anti-modern fundamentalist Islamic republic. Khomeini stirred the anti-Western frenzy of his followers to storm the U.S. Embassy in Tehran. Shi'ites held 52 American Embassy personnel as hostages for over a year.

Shi'ite leaders in Iran have also aided terrorist groups in Lebanon. One of these groups, the **Islamic Jihad** was responsible for a disastrous suicide bombing in 1982. The attack resulted in the deaths of over 200 U.S. Marines who were part of a U.N. peace-keeping mission. Other groups began taking Western hostages randomly in the 1980's. The objective was to force the exchange of terrorist prisoners taken by Israel. Most hostages were held until 1991 when Middle East peace negotiations aided in their release.

Europe

Terrorism is not confined to the Middle East. The long struggle for power between Catholic and Protestant in Northern Ireland groups has seen much violence and denial of human rights. The **Provisional Wing of the Irish Republican Army** employs terrorism to force the British to give up control of the area. The "Provos" have been responsible for attacks on the British Prime Minister's residence and London airports and subways. Radical Protestant groups such as the **Ulster Defense League** retaliate with executions, bombings, and armed attacks on Catholic neighborhoods in Belfast. In a 1985 treaty, Britain agreed to allow Ireland to intervene in human rights cases, but the terrorist war continues. To date, it has claimed over 2000 lives.

Additional Information on War and Peace

Consult your text on various wars and acts of terrorism. In *N&N's Global Studies Review Text,* more information on can be found on
Arab-Israeli Wars [pgs. 210-212]
Boer War [pg. 33]
Civil War in China [pgs. 104-106]
Civil wars in Kampuchea and Laos [pgs. 75-76]
Civil War in Lebanon [pgs. 222-223]
German and Italian wars of unification [pg. 257]
Iran-Iraq War [pgs. 214-215]
Korean War [pg. 120]
Opium War [pgs. 102-103]
Russo-Japanese War [pgs. 134-135]
Sino-Japanese War [pg. 134]
Vietnam War [pgs. 74-74, 120, 291]
World War I [pgs. 262-264]
War in Afghanistan [pgs. 223-224]

Questions

Base your answer to question 1 on the map at the right and on your knowledge of social studies.

Europe in World War I

CENTRAL POWERS

ALLIED POWERS

British Naval Blockade

NEUTRALS

1   Which problem of the Central Powers does the map show?
    1   They had no access to the sea.
    2   It was necessary for them to fight on two fronts.
    3   There was no common border with Russia.
    4   They were widely dispersed across Europe.

2   A basic cause of war in late 19th and early 20th Century Europe was
    1   nationalism
    2   slavery
    3   religious fundamentalism
    4   ideological conflict

3   Which of the developments in technology is correctly associated with the war during which it was invented?
   1   World War I - tank   3   Hundred Years War - missiles
   2   Korean War - poison gas   4   World War II - submarine

4   The primary aim of the concept of balance of power in Europe during the 19th Century was to
   1   eliminate war as foreign policy
   2   prevent domination by any one country
   3   create equal land and sea forces within each nation
   4   divide Europe under two equal military powers

5   During the 1930's, a joint act of appeasement by the British and the French was
   1   signing a treaty with Germany to outlaw nuclear weapons
   2   giving Czechoslovakia's Sudetenland to Germany
   3   entering into a defensive alliance with the United States
   4   supporting independence for German colonies in Africa

6   Which statement about the actions of the Congress of Vienna is accurate?
   1   Pre-Napoleonic rulers were not restored to power.
   2   The nations of Italy and Germany were created.
   3   The forces of nationalism and democracy were largely ignored.
   4   No provisions were made to preserve the settlement.

7   The Treaty of Versailles signed by Germany at the Paris Peace Conference provided for
   1   freedom of the seas
   2   removal of trade barriers
   3   establishment of the United Nations
   4   limits on the size of the German military

8   Which belief would be shared by terrorist groups around the globe?
   1   Membership in the United Nations is worthless
   2   Communism will spread throughout the world without armed conflict
   3   Socialism inevitably leads to dictatorship
   4   History shows the value of forceful action

9   After World War I, there was extensive change in
   1   the number of independent nations in Europe
   2   methods of conducting international trade
   3   the governments of Great Britain and France
   4   the number of colonies in Africa

10   Which was a result of both World War I and World War II?
   1   Nations tried to avoid war through international peace organizations.
   2   Ideological differences ceased to be causes of international conflict.
   3   Political revolutions were banned.
   4   Colonial empires were strengthened to keep peace.

11   Both World War I and World War II were caused by
   1   the assassination of Archduke Franz Ferdinand
   2   an increase in nationalism
   3   a serious economic depression
   4   appeasement policies of the democratic nations

12 Nearly all wars cause interactions of people which have led to
1 cultural diffusion
2 resolution of religious differences
3 loss of technological progress
4 long lasting peace settlements

13 Which statement best describes the relationship between World War I and the Russian Revolution?
1 WW I created conditions within Russia that helped trigger a revolution.
2 WW I postponed the Russian Revolution by restoring confidence in the Tsar.
3 The Russian Revolution inspired the Russian people to win WW I.
4 WW I gave the Tsar's army the needed experience to suppress the Russian Revolution.

Base your answers to questions 14 on the cartoon below and on your knowledge of social studies.

14 Which statement best illustrates the meaning of the cartoon?
1 Lebanese Christians are winning the power struggle.
2 Urban slums threaten the Lebanese economy.
3 Terrorism by religious groups has destroyed Lebanon.
4 Terrorists' primitive weapons are ineffective.

Model Essay

1 Wars have played major roles in affecting the economic, social, and political development of the global community.

Statements on War

Wars lead to technological development.
Wars are frequently caused by the same factors.
Peace settlements at the end of one war often cause a later war.
Human rights are often violated during wars.

Select *three* of the statements below, and for *each* one selected use *two* examples to assess its accuracy. [5,5,5]

Pre-writing Strategy: Before you begin to write your answer in full sentences, lay out your preliminary information on the grid below. [Note that the question does not stop you from using the same war more than once.]

Peace settlements at the end of one war often cause a later war.	
Example 1: The peace settlement established at the Congress of Vienna at the end of the Napoleonic Wars ignored the newly spread forces of nationalism and democracy. People in areas such as Belgium and the Italian states were not allowed national independence and former colonies were restored in countries such as Spain without the consent of the people in them. As a consequence, a series of revolutions accompanied by fighting broke out in the 1820's, 1830's, and 1848.	*Example 1:*

Wars are frequently caused by the same factors.	
Example 1: Nationalism was a major cause of the Franco-Prussian War. The desire of many of the German states to be unified led Prussian Chancellor Bismarck to actively seek war with France to unify the Germans against a foreign enemy. The result was the establishment of the German Empire and further wounding of French pride which played a role in the nationalism leading to World War I.	*Example 2:*

Human rights are often violated during wars.	
Example 1: The WW II genocide (Holocaust) conducted by Hitler against the Jews is the best example of the violation of human rights during wartime. By the order of the Nazis, six million Jews were killed in extermination camps such as Auschwitz.	*Example 2:*

After completing the grid, write out your answers in three separate paragraphs, using complete sentences.

Additional Practice Essays

It is suggested that you design and complete your own grid layouts as "pre-writing" exercises for these additional essays.

2   Since 1945, many nations and areas have experienced major internal conflicts between groups that have disagreed on various issues.

Nations/Areas

Korea   Lebanon
Northern Ireland   Philippines
Poland   Vietnam

Select *one* nation or area from the list above.

a   Identify a major internal conflict that has taken place in the nation or area. [3]

b   Within the nation or area, identify *two* groups which have been involved in the internal conflict and explain the position *each* group has taken in that conflict. [3,3]

c   Describe the current status of the conflict or the extent to which the conflict has been resolved. [6]

3   In the course of global history, various groups have resorted to terrorist activities to achieve their goals.

Group

Palestinian Liberation Organization
Provisional Wing of the Irish Republican Army
Shi'ite Islamic Jihad in Lebanon
Mau Mau in Kenya
Sikh Nationalist Extremists in India

Select *three* groups. For *each* group, discuss the conflict that has led the group to use terrorism, and indicate a terrorist activity of the group. [5,5,5.]

LESSON 2

Over-Population

Demographers (scholars who study and predict the effects of population changes in global regions) tell us that many global issues such as overcrowding, depletion of natural resources, pollution of the environment, and political unrest are a direct result of overpopulation and the uneven distribution of the people on the Earth. This is most evident in the overcrowded conditions in many of the world's urban centers. More than 80% of these are located in the lesser developed nations.

World Issue 1

Rapid Urban Growth in Developing Nations

Location   — Urban

In 1800, only 3% of the world's peoples lived in cities. Today, over 40% live in urban centers. Most of this increase is due to the steady migration of rural villagers seeking better economic opportunities in cities.

Much of the massive growth of cities in Latin America, Asia, and Africa has taken place in the last twenty years. The United Nations now expects that by the year 2000, seventeen of the world's twenty largest cities will exist in the Third World. Mexico City and Sao Paulo (Brazil) will become the largest with projected populations of 25 million. Many smaller cities, such as Karachi (Pakistan), Lagos (Nigeria), and Jakarta (Indonesia), will be expanding at faster growth rates than the Latin American cities.

Why

The rising birth rate in many of the lesser developed nations contributes to this problem of urban growth. It is partially due to improved medical technology and religious objections to birth control.

Results

A cause of over-stressed urban environments is the migration of rural families into the cities because of drought and famine. This population explosion stretches these cities' scarce resources to the limit.

Urban slums are more prevalent in the less developed nations. Urban housing has not kept up with the population movement. The United Nations estimates that more than half of the urban population in the Third World Nations live in slum conditions.

Tragic environmental disasters are forecast. Smog, lack of clean water, and inadequate sewerage will cause widespread epidemics. In Calcutta (India) more than 60% of the residents suffer from breathing problems. Residents of these "megacities" may start dying in vast numbers.

Future ?

Can the urban overpopulation problems be solved? Governments continually warn the people but have been unable to restrict population movement.

Regional Urban Growth

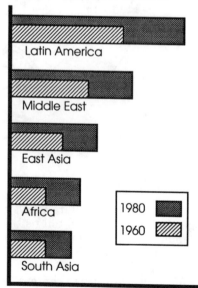

0   10   20   30   40   50   60   70   80

Percent of Population in Cities

Source: World Bank, 1983

World
Issue 2

India's Population ~790 Mi
Problems ~food

The population issue has been one of India's most persistent problems. For decades, the Indian subcontinent has struggled to support a population increasing at one of the highest rates in the world.

Why

The most crucial problem facing India is supplying adequate food. Land reform programs have given more small farmers land, but subsistence agriculture cannot supply the kinds of harvests India needs annually. More than half the farms are one acre or less.

Results

In 1952, India was the first country to adopt a **nationwide family planning** program. However, there has been a steady population increase. 1

Reproduction of an
Indian government
poster to encourage
lower birth rates.

PRACTISE FAMILY PLANNING

2 Improved medical care has increased life expectancy. There are also traditional and religious reasons for overpopulation.

3 In labor-intensive agriculture, large families have always been a necessity. Technological progress in farming has lagged and farm families continue to grow. Family loyalty is still strong. Those children who migrate to India's cities are expected to send contributions home. Hinduism teaches that having children is virtuous.

4 The continued population growth affects the economy, urban development, and the quality of life in India. The country does not have the natural or financial resources to provide the consumer goods for a rapidly expanding population. Unemployment is high. Annual per capita income in 1990 was only 250 dollars.

5 Rural poverty has caused a massive migration to urban areas. Since 1960, cities have grown at three times the rate of rural areas. Crowded slums, poor sanitation, inadequate housing, disease, and crime abound.

6 At present, India is producing enough grain to feed its population. Total production has risen dramatically. **"The Green Revolution"** has helped with better land management, improved fertilizers, high yield seed, pesti-

cides, and modern equipment. However, the rapid rate of population growth has actually caused per capita production to fall.

India's continued population growth (280 million to over 1 billion in the next 30 years) will strain the nation's already limited resources and lower the **per capita GNP** (what the nation annually produces divided by the total population). Starvation and environmental disasters will certainly result.

Future

Can India solve its population problem? The key is the government's ability to achieve success with its family planning programs and in changing old social and religious patterns.

Population Problems in Developing Nations in Africa

World Issue **3**

Where

Nations such as Nigeria and Kenya have extremely high population growth rates. Lagos, Nigeria's capital, with a population of 7 million, is twenty times larger than it was in 1960 when the country received its independence from Great Britain. It is estimated that Sub-Saharan Africa's population will double by the year 2010.

why

① Medical advances have lowered death rates. As in India, traditional beliefs are also a cause. In rural areas, there are pressures for large families. Many children are needed for primitive, labor-intensive agriculture. Many parents also look upon their children as a support system in their old age.

② Growth can be traced to the industrial economic development of the colonial era and to modern buildings and services created by today's nationalist leaders who wish to showcase their achievements.

Results

1. Urban growth invites huge waves of migrants from rural areas. They flow into the cities searching for jobs and creating severe urban congestion and breakdowns in essential services (transportation, housing, sewage).

2. Unlike many Sub-Saharan African nations, Nigeria has large oil reserves. This helps the economy, but the revenues are not transferred into agricultural development. People continue to starve. The focus on oil exports also makes the country too dependent on the world petroleum market. When prices decline as they did in the 1980's, the whole economy suffers. Nigeria's annual per capita GNP declined from 710 dollars in 1985 to 650 dollars in 1989. (U.S. per capita is over 15,000 dollars.) At the same time, the population continues to grow, making the problems worse.

3. When the unskilled rural worker is unable to do the jobs associated with modern industrial technology, high unemployment results. Most of the recent migrants to the cities live in slum areas. These depressing shanty towns are on the fringe of thriving business districts and wealthy neighborhoods. However, as long as cities continue to be the industrial hubs and the central seats of government, they offer chances for a better life. It will be very difficult to control population shifts from rural to urban areas.

Additional Information on Population

Consult your text on population, overpopulation, and urban problems in the various regions of the world. In *N&N's Global Studies Review Text,* more information on can be found on

India's population problems [pg. 72]
Africa's problems [pg. 44]
World population pressures [pg. 348]

Questions

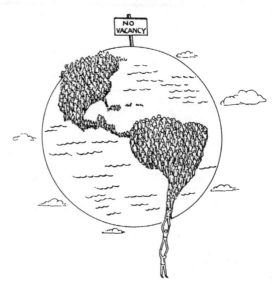

Answer question 1 based on the cartoon and your knowledge of social studies.

1   What is the cartoonist's message?
   1   The oceans can provide enough food for everyone.
   2   The most populous areas are along sea coasts.
   3   The oceans are the most polluted parts of the planet.
   4   The world is becoming overcrowded.

2   Which contributes to South Asia's population problem?
   1   overproduction of staple crops
   2   the rapid pace of industrial production
   3   changing roles of women
   4   decreasing mortality rates

3   Many global issues, such as overcrowding and pollution are a direct result of
   1   high unemployment
   2   farm based economies
   3   overpopulation
   4   the imbalance of world trade

4   The major factor contributing to rapid growth of urban centers in the 20th century is the
   1   search for economic opportunity
   2   traditional influence of village elders
   3   peoples' love of crowded conditions
   4   development of the computer

5   A major reason for higher birth rates in the Third World is
   1   promotion of birth control programs
   2   improved medical facilities
   3   overeducation in hygiene
   4   military power depends on large populations

6   A major cause of the development of shanty towns has been
   1   a breakdown of essential urban services
   2   increased employment in cities
   3   increased social mobility
   4   rural to urban population shifts

7   Unlike the United States, the internal migration patterns in most Latin
     American nations is from
     1   rural to urban areas
     2   cities to suburbs
     3   urban to rural regions
     4   suburbs to rural regions

8   Currently, which situation in developing nations of South and Southeast
     Asia hurts efforts to raise living standards?
     1   continued high rates of population growth
     2   the rapid pace of industrialization
     3   the "Green Revolution"
     4   nationalistic rejection of Western technology

9   The most crucial problem facing India is
     1   protection of oil resources
     2   communist rebellions
     3   breakup of the caste system
     4   supplying adequate food

*Base your answer to question 10 on the graphs below and on your knowledge
of social studies.*

BIRTH AND DEATH RATES
IN ECONOMICALLY DEVELOPED AND ECONOMICALLY DEVELOPING COUNTRIES
1850–1977

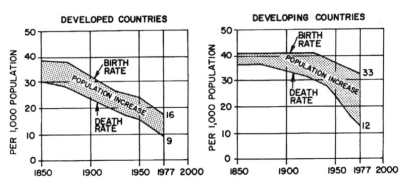

RATE OF POPULATION INCREASE = BIRTH RATE — DEATH RATE
Source: United Nations Population Division

10   Which statement is best supported by the information in the graphs?
     1   Population in both developed and developing countries increases at
          the same rate.
     2   By the year 2000, the developing countries will reach the point of
          zero population growth.
     3   Population growth since 1900 has largely been due to a drop in the
          death rate.
     4   Population growth since 1900 has largely been due to an increase in
          the birth rate.

Model Essay

(Note: Most often, population problems are included as one of the choices in more general questions on world problems.)

1 Demographic projections for the next thirty years show that there will be alarming growth in developing nations.

30-Year Population Projection		
Nation	*1987 Population*	*2021 Population*
Bangladesh	105 million	210 million
Brazil	144 million	242 million
China	1,060 million	1,418 million
India	790 million	1,213 million
Indonesia	170 million	265 million
Iran	48 million	95 million
Japan	122 million	135 million
Mexico	82 million	148 million
Nigeria	107 million	315 million
Tanzania	24 million	75 million
United States	242 million	310 million

a Explain *two* reasons why the chart above shows such a dramatic increase in the population figures for developing nations. [5]

b Select *two* developing nations from the chart above and for *each* nation selected explain a problem caused by population growth. (A different problem must be used for each nation.) [5, 5]

Pre-writing Strategy: Before you begin to write your answer in full sentences, lay out your preliminary information on the grids on the next page to be sure you have all the required parts of the answer.

a) Dramatic Increase in the Population of Developing Nations	
Cause 1:	Cause 2:

b) Problem Caused by Population Growth	
Developing Nation:	
India	
Nigeria	

After completing the grid, write out your answer. Label the parts "a" and "b." Be sure to write complete sentences.

Additional Practice Essays

It is suggested that you design and complete your own grid layouts as "pre-writing" exercises for these additional essays.

2   Because of rapid population growth, India's government has attempted reform and social change since independence was granted by Great Britain in 1948.

 a   Discuss *one* reform India's government has attempted to deal with the problem of rapid population growth. [5]

 b   Discuss *two* reasons why governmental reforms have not been able to succeed in India. [5,5]

3   Overpopulation in many developing African nations has contributed to widespread poverty.

 a   Describe the causes of overpopulation in *one* specific African nation. [5]

 b   Explain how urbanization has affected the population problem. [5]

 c   Show how the problems indicated in *a* and *b* affect African agricultural production. [5]

LESSON 3

Hunger and Poverty

Most people in the developed world lack any true conception of the extent of poverty in the Third World. The people of the developing nations constitute nearly 75% of the world's population. For the majority of them, living conditions are barely tolerable. Survival is a constant struggle.

Where work is available, it is at a mere **subsistence level**. Health and sanitary conditions defy the imagination of a person born and raised in a developed nation.

Unlike the United States, these countries usually have no governmental programs such as the Social Security system or unemployment compensation. If family wage earners are victims of a disabling sickness or death, malnutrition and starvation befalls the family.

No "Safety Net"

World Issue 1

Causes of Hunger in Africa

In a world of plenty, why do so many go hungry? In the Third World regions, such as Africa, our first instinct is to blame overpopulation. That is partly true. However, a closer examination indicates it is not the only reason. Among the other reasons are:

- Lack of adequate water resources
- Soil erosion from deforestation and desertification
- Civil wars in Ethiopia, Sudan, and Mozambique that have seen the withholding of food supplies used as a weapon
- Expensive and wasteful government projects which misdirect economic resources
- Frequent natural disasters beyond human control (droughts, floods, earthquakes)
- Lack of a modern **infrastructure** (transportation-communication network) to effectively distribute goods
- Large corporate cash crop farms which produce products for export to the developed nations (coffee, cotton, peanuts) which are profitable, but do not meet local people's needs for food
- Resistance to technological training by traditionalist farmers (see "Green Revolution" in section 4 and in the "Population" section)

The land is not yielding the food supplies to alleviate hunger. Most of the African nations have become dependent on foreign aid and food subsidies from grain surpluses of the Western world. Technical training and financial assistance being brought in from the outside world must be used more prudently. Urban growth must be controlled, or there will be a continual breakdown of needed services. The problem of perpetual hunger cannot be solved until all of these issues are addressed. African nations become more vulnerable as world grain reserves continue to fall because of adverse weather conditions related to the **Greenhouse Effect**. (see Lesson 6: Environment)

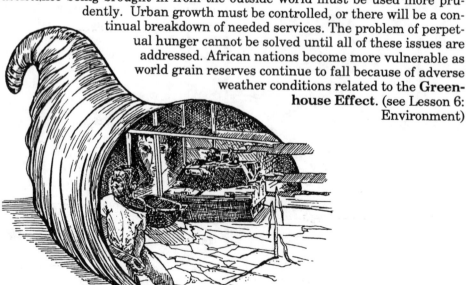

Natural & Human Causes for Poverty in Bangladesh

In South Asia, the newly independent nation of Bangladesh is an example of the never-ending cycle of poverty. When the monsoon–carried rains flood the low-lying plains of the Brahmaputra and Ganges Rivers, a severe famine often results. In the 1970's, floods repeatedly destroyed vital farmlands. In 1985, a massive tidal wave left nearly 50% of the Bengali farmers landless.

Besides natural disasters, a combination of human conditions contribute to placing Bangladesh among the poorest nations in the world. A statistical comparison to other Asian nations gives us some idea of the extent of this nation's poverty:

Socio-Economic Status of Asian Countries			
Country	**Per Capita GNP**	**Life Expectancy**	**Infant Mortality** (per 1,000 births)
Bangladesh	113	49	140
India	260	52	101
Philippines	589	63	53
Japan	10,266	77	6
Thailand	770	63	53
Country	**Percent Urban Population**	**Percent Literate**	**Birth Rate** (per 1,000 people)
Bangladesh	12	25	45
India	22	36	33
Philippines	37	88	31
Japan	76	99	12
Thailand	15	86	30

While the statistics on the chart indicate a very low standard of living for Bangladesh, they do not tell the entire story. Since its independence from Pakistan in 1971, Bangladesh has been politically unstable and scarred by episodes of widespread violence. For most of its eighteen years, the nation has been under martial law and governed by a succession of military rulers.

Natural disasters, political unrest, decline in importance of its major exports, widespread illiteracy, and overpopulation have combined to make Bangladesh one of the poorest nations on Earth.

Political Causes of Poverty in Latin America

World Issue **3**

In Latin America, poverty has existed since the days of Spanish and Portuguese colonial rule. Under the **hacienda system**, the crown gave the nobles huge land grants which became plantations. This created an unfair hereditary distribution of land. Today 10% of the people control 90% of the land in Latin America.

Land Control - Dependecy

Millions of **campesinos** (agricultural laborers) work the very large farms. In exchange, they are given little pay and tiny plots of the poorest land. Most of the campesinos are Indians, Blacks, Mulattos, or Mestizos who must use their own primitive tools and farming methods. They have little chance for education and rarely rise above the subsistence level of existence.

The problem is compounded by Latin American economic leaders' favoring single cash products for export (coffee, bananas, sugar cane, or cattle). This kind of economy only benefits the richer landholders. It does nothing to increase domestic food supplies.

Hope for the future of the Latin American poor remains with those political leaders who promise **land reform** by breaking up the hacienda system and redistributing property. When reform leaders are elected, the wealthy landholders sabotage their programs. The wealthy landowners pressure bureaucrats to hinder administration of the reforms.

"The Green Revolution" A Solution for Poverty?

World Issue **4**

Land Reform - Insufficient

In some countries such as Mexico, even when land reform does take place, it is unsuccessful. Campesinos lack the education, technology, and financial resources to lift themselves above the subsistence levels. The programs must have a broader focus than just the breaking up of the huge cash crop farms and ranches.

One hope is that the **Green Revolution** (organized attempts to focus the scientific and technological advances of agriculture on the problems of less developed countries) may provide that broader focus. To maximize the Green Revolution's potential for relieving Third World poverty and hunger, expensive irrigation methods and petrochemical fertilizers must be employed. Funding is limited.

Major agricultural advances have been made on the lands of richer classes of farmers, but have not helped the poor. In some cases, the frustrations of seeing the rich advance has led to class warfare. (Nicaragua's communist revolution was fueled by such resentment.)

The application of Green Revolution techniques to India's rice and wheat production has dramatically raised production to a point where the country's population has begun to receive an adequate food supply.

Other Third World nations have not been as successful as India. Most rely on the developed nations for financial aid, supplies of fertilizer, and other advanced farm technology. They are often subjected to economic dependence on other countries. This dependence keeps their trade unbalanced.

The Green Revolution helps increase the world's food supplies. However, to continue the struggle, people must recognize that reallocation of resources is necessary to cut down waste and corruption. This means changing political and social attitudes on a global scale.

Why Are Hunger and Poverty a Global Concern?

World Issue 5

Less than a decade ago, President Carter of the United States said, "We need to share a responsibility for solving problems, not divide the blame for ignoring them." He echoed the claims of most of the world's food experts who stress the need for international cooperation.

During the famine years, there has been a global response from governments and private organizations for relief. However, the real ongoing problems cannot be solved by periodic gestures. There is a need for long-range measures that will not merely alleviate problems, but begin to solve them.

In the mid-1970's, **OPEC** raised world oil prices dramatically. Because of the resulting high prices not only for fuel but also for manufactured goods and services, many of the lesser developed countries petitioned the United Nations for long term assistance for their situation.

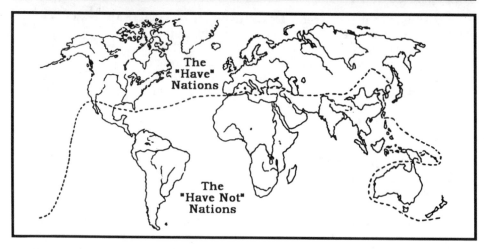

Third World nations asked for:

- Cancellation or reduction of debts
- Increased foreign aid
- More technology and advisors at lower prices
- Higher prices for their exports

With the developed nations feeling the economic pressures of rising oil prices themselves, they were not in a generous mood to receive these requests. However, United Nations officials went even further than the less developed nations wanted in pointing out the dire need for international cooperation as opposed to national self-interest. The U.N. initiated a program which included:

- Long term low interest loans from oil rich nations for immediate famine relief
- Equalization of prices on a direct exchange of the developed nations' technological equipment and skills for less developed nations' raw materials

These proposals were greeted with enthusiasm by the "Have" nations. They perceive themselves as sacrificing too much and receiving too little in return. The problems will deepen in the "Have Not" nations before the 25% who control the world's economic resources will heed the requests of the U.N. Perhaps when the "Haves" see the imbalance as a threat to their existence, the world will deal decisively with global hunger and poverty.

Additional Information on Hunger and Poverty

Consult your text on poverty and hunger in the various regions. In *N&N's Global Studies Review Text,* more information on can be found on

Africa's problems [pg. 44]

World hunger problems [pg. 349]

Questions

1   Subsistence level existence means
     1   barely producing enough for one's own immediate use
     2   rapid industrial production
     3   large scale cash crop production
     4   the new lifestyle emerging in urban centers

2   Which factor had the greatest influence on food production in
     Bangladesh?
     1   switch to cash crop farms
     2   natural disasters
     3   rising oil prices
     4   development of the computer

3   Which factor is most common to nations in which poverty and hunger
     are major problems?
     1   high standard of living
     2   inadequate infrastructures
     3   high literacy rates
     4   low birth rates

4   Which of the following news headlines best illustrates the major cause of
     poverty in Africa?
     1   Ethiopian Leaders Withhold Famine Relief Food Supplies To Starve
          Out Rebels.
     2   Religious Groups Oppose Taking Aid From United Nations.
     3   High Speed Trains Now Connect Major Cities in East Africa.
     4   Monsoon Flooding Ruins Crops Again in Ethiopia.

5   Several regions in Africa, such as the Sahel, have experienced famines
     caused by
     1   devastating tidal waves
     2   massive earthquakes
     3   widespread drought
     4   volcanic eruptions

6   In Bangladesh, current figures indicate a 26% rate of literacy. This
     contributes to poverty because the labor force has little
     1   capability of dealing with modern technology
     2   political stability
     3   need for electronic equipment
     4   desire for territorial expansion

7   In order to prevent hunger and poverty in the underdeveloped nations,
     these nations must
     1   develop their own industries
     2   control rampant population growth
     3   conduct wars for territorial expansion
     4   develop nuclear energy sources

8   Imbalance in food supplies occurred in the middle 1970's when the
     OPEC cartel raised oil prices because modern agricultural production
     depends on
     1   cheap energy and petrochemical fertilizers
     2   United Nations' direction of food distribution
     3   military defense of the Mediterranean
     4   grains produced in the Middle East and North Africa

*Answer question 9 and 10 based on the graphs below and on your knowledge
of social studies.*

Key Elements Involved in Global Food Production

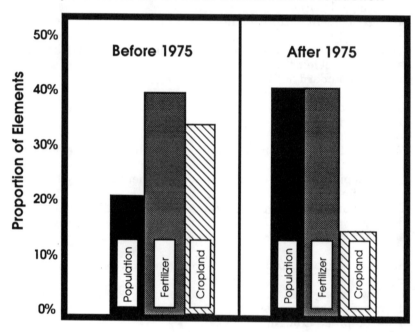

9   Which describes the change in the relationship of the elements of food
     production?
     1   Fertilizer production is not sufficient for the amount of land.
     2   Population appears to have outgrown the land needed to feed it.
     3   There has never been enough fertilizer in proportion to cropland.
     4   There is too much cropland under production to feed the population.

10   What happens if this new trend in the proportion of cropland to those of
     fertilizer and population continues?
     1   Food will become less expensive in general.
     2   Food surpluses will become widespread.
     3   Food increases will lead directly to overpopulation.
     4   Food shortages will become more common.

Model Essay

(Note: Most often, poverty and hunger problems are usually included as one of the choices in questions on world problems.)

1   Developing nations suffer from hunger and poverty for a variety of reasons

Reasons
- Environmental mismanagement
- Political instability
- Wasteful government projects
- Frequent natural disasters
- Lack of a modern infrastructure
- Large corporate cash crop farms
- Resistance to technological training

    a   Select *two* reasons from the list above. For *each* reason selected, tell how that reason contributes to hunger and poverty in developing nations. [6,6]

    b   Since its creation, the United Nations has attempted to coordinate the efforts of the "Have" (developed) nations to help the "Have Not" (developing) nations. Cite a *specific* idea or program the U.N. has tried to coordinate to aid developing nations and discuss its success or failure. [3]

Pre-writing Strategy: Before you begin to write your answer in full sentences, lay out your preliminary information on the grids below and on the next page to be sure you have all the required parts of the answer.

a) **Suffering from Hunger and Poverty**	
Reasons: Large corporate cash crop farms	*Third World Poverty Causes:*
Frequent natural disasters	

b) U.N. Program to Help the Developing Nations	
U.N. Program: Green Revolution	*Program Success/Failure:*

After completing the grid, write out your answers to the "a" and "b" sections in full sentences.

Additional Practice Essay

It is suggested that you design and complete your own grid layout as a "pre-writing" exercise for this additional essay.

2   The Green Revolution, introduced to the world's developing countries in the 1960's, brought dramatic increases in crop yields.

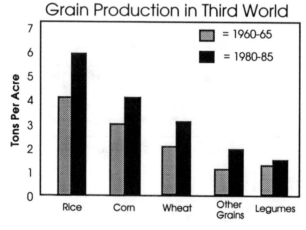

Grain Production in Third World

a   According to the graph, which *two* grains have seen the greatest increase in yield? [3]

b   What are some of the advanced agricultural techniques used in the Green Revolution? [3]

c   Choose *one* nation in Latin America, Asia, or Africa that has successfully applied Green Revolution technology and explain how it has helped that nation. [6]

d   Why hasn't the Green Revolution been more successful? [3]

LESSON 4

Political and Economic Refugees

Why → Refugees ① war ② natural disasters ③ Industrialization

The large numbers of political and economic refugees has been and remains a major problem in the world today. It involves the resettlement of groups uprooted by wars, natural disasters, and the process of industrialization. Large scale migrations of people cause stress and conflict throughout affected global regions. One of the problems in host countries is the increased demand on already limited resources (scarcity). Other people, in less affected areas of the world, can empathize with the sufferings of such refugee groups.

European Refugees Help Zionists Establish Israel

Where — Palestine /Israel (handwritten)

Zionism, a movement for the creation of a Jewish homeland, was founded in 1897 by Theodore Herzl. Zionism gained momentum when Britain, hoping for Jewish support on World War I, issued the Balfour Declaration in 1917. This document supported the establishment of a national home for the Jewish people in Palestine. *(Holy Land)* (handwritten)

Who (handwritten)

Encouraged by the Balfour declaration, European Jews began to migrate to the Middle East **mandates** (administrative territories) assigned to the British after the war by the League of Nations. Hitler's behavior in the 1930's caused the pace of the Jewish migration into Palestine to increase.

As this migration built momentum in the 1930's, Arab inhabitants of Palestine felt threatened by the European refugees. The British compounded the problem by attempting to guarantee the same kind of autonomous rule to the Arabs in Palestine as they had the Jews. At the same time, they passed entry quotas to stem the tide of Jewish migration.

Holocaust (handwritten)

At the end of World War II, when the atrocities of the Nazi **Holocaust** against the Jews became known, empathy for the Zionist cause began to build. Support grew rapidly for the Zionist insurgent movement. The British withdrew troops from the region and turned the problem over to the United Nations. Fighting broke out between Palestinian Arabs and Jewish refugees. A fragile truce agreement was finally achieved by the U.N. in 1948 after fierce fighting had gone in favor of the Zionists forces. The state of Israel was recognized as a new nation shortly afterward.

Palestinian Refugees

Perhaps the greatest conflict in the Middle East centers on the possession of the land once known as Palestine. In 1948, when the area became recognized as Israel, one million Palestinian Arabs were displaced. These people came to be resettled in political refugee camps in neighboring Arab nations. Syria, Jordan, and Egypt were ill-prepared to absorb these refugees.

The camps still exist today, holding some 700 thousand people. The camps have also become controversial because they provide training camps for Palestinian guerrilla fighters and terrorist groups.

Beyond the camps, there are an estimated three million Palestinian Arab refugees scattered throughout the Middle East. Their leaders demand evacuation of Israeli-held territory and the formation of a sovereign Palestinian nation on the West Bank of the Jordan River.

4M.

Economic Refugees in the Latin American Barrios

of Urban

World Issue 3

why

Seventy percent of all Latin Americans live in urban centers. Since World War II, Latin American cities have grown twice as fast as those in other global regions. The growth has been largely due to poor rural migrants moving into the cities for better economic opportunity. The poor of Latin America have become economic refugees in their own countries. ①

Results

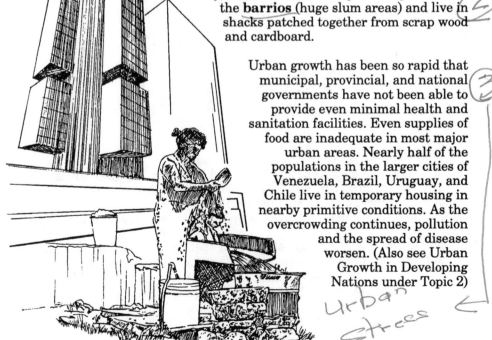

Great contrast between rich and poor is evident in cities such as Caracas, Lima, Rio de Janeiro, Mexico City, and São Paulo. The poor are packed into the **barrios** (huge slum areas) and live in shacks patched together from scrap wood and cardboard. ②

Urban growth has been so rapid that municipal, provincial, and national governments have not been able to provide even minimal health and sanitation facilities. Even supplies of food are inadequate in most major urban areas. Nearly half of the populations in the larger cities of Venezuela, Brazil, Uruguay, and Chile live in temporary housing in nearby primitive conditions. As the overcrowding continues, pollution and the spread of disease worsen. (Also see Urban Growth in Developing Nations under Topic 2) ③

Urban stress

Additional Information on Refugees

Consult your text on refugees. In *N&N's Global Studies Review Text,* more information on can be found on

African shanty towns [pg. 351]
Lebanese Refugees [pgs. 222-223]
Political refugees on Taiwan [pg. 106]
Economic refugees in Western Europe today [pg. 277]
Vietnamese 'boat people' [pg.77]
Arab-Israeli Conflict [pgs. 206, 209-210, 223]

Questions

Base your answer to question 1 on the cartoon and on your knowledge of social studies.

SEND ME YOUR PROGRAMMERS, YOUR SCIENTISTS, YOUR ELECTRICAL ENGINEERS......SEND YOUR RESEARCHERS, TECHNICIANS, YOUR COMPUTER SYSTEMS SPECIALISTS....SEND YOUR

U.S. HIGH TECH DRIVE

1   Which best states the main idea of the cartoon?
   1   There is a surplus of highly trained people in foreign countries.
   2   Nations primarily welcome refugees with technical skills.
   3   Robots will one day rule the world.
   4   Natural population growth in industrialized nations is small.

2   The founding of the nation of Israel in 1948 provided a partial solution to the problems of Jewish refugees. At the same time, it created a problem of
   1   Palestinian refugees
   2   Zionism
   3   overcrowding in barrios
   4   urban growth

Base your answer to question 3 on the graph and on your knowledge of social studies.

Regional Urban Growth

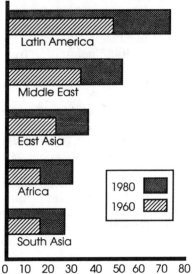

Percent of Population in Cities
Source: World Bank, 1983

3 Which statement about regional growth is most clearly supported by the graph?
1 The percent of Africans living in cities has remained relatively unchanged over the decades shown.
2 The Middle East and East Asia have experienced a dramatic decline in urban population.
3 The percent of Latin Americans living in cities is higher than in the other global regions shown in both time periods.
4 Latin America has the world's highest rural and urban birth rate.

4 Cultural diversity in a global region is often a result of
1 hostile governmental actions toward political and economic refugees
2 the totalitarian policies of governments
3 intense competition of people for food supplies
4 migrations into an area by groups of refugees

5 A major problem for Latin American countries has been the
1 power of the rural poor
2 migration of rural poor to cities
3 domination of military by the leaders of the rural poor
4 widespread reform of educational systems

6 In underdeveloped areas of the globe, one major reason why refugees migrate is to
1 gain more political power
2 escape the use of dangerous chemical fertilizers
3 find better employment opportunities
4 enjoy more sophisticated forms of entertainment

7 Since the end of World War II, the Middle East has experienced a considerable refugee problem, primarily because of
1 Egypt's insistence on building dams on the Nile
2 the establishment of the nation of Israel
3 annexation of colonies by Western European nations
4 the construction of the Baghdad-Berlin railroad

8 Which is generally characteristic of a nation undergoing industrial change?
1 less opportunity for social mobility
2 few opportunities for capital investment
3 increased reliance on extended families for labor
4 shifts in population from rural to urban areas

9 Shanty towns are being created in cities in developing nations because of the
1 limited funding for basic housing for poor newcomers
2 need for new workers
3 ethnocentric policies of municipal governments
4 need for refugee camps

10 Many Arab nations have been hostile toward Israel because it
1 controls the Suez Canal
2 refuses to share its nuclear power
3 tries to convert Muslims to Judaism
4 occupies territories formerly held by Arab peoples

Model Essay

1 Throughout history, people have become refugees seeking to escape political and economic conflicts and upheavals that have altered their lives.

Refugee Groups

Vietnamese [1950's - 1970's]
Palestinians [since 1948]
Cambodians [1970's - 1980's]
French [1790's]
Jews [20th century]
Latin Americans [since 1945]

Choose *three* of the groups listed above and for *each* one,

· Explain the conflict or upheaval they experienced.

· Discuss how the conflict or upheaval has affected their lives. [5,5,5]

Pre-writing Strategy: Before writing your answer in sentences, lay out preliminary information on the grid format on the next page.

Refugee Group: **Cambodians (1970's)**	
Conflict/Upheaval: After World War II, the collapse of the French colonial government in Cambodia opened a civil war between pro-west and radical Khmer Rouge communist groups. It intensified with the 1973 withdrawal of U.S. troops from neighboring Vietnam. The Khmer Rouge victory in 1975 led to renaming the country Kampuchea. Massive purges, executions, and forced resettlements followed. An estimated 4 million lives were lost.	*How Lives Affected:*

Refugee Group: **Latin Americans (since 1945)**	
Conflict/Upheaval:	*How Lives Affected:* Rural migrants are forced to live in the poorest and most unhealthy conditions in the barrios of cities such as La Paz, Bogota, Santiago, and São Paulo.

Refugee Group: **Palestinians (since 1948)**	
Conflict/Upheaval:	*How Lives Affected:* Over one million Arabs were uprooted and went to live in refugee camps surrounding Israel. Opposition and terrorist groups such as the PLO continue to operate as guerrilla forces from the refugee camps.

After completing the grid, write out your answers in three separate paragraphs, using complete sentences.

Additional Practice Essays

It is suggested that you design and complete your own grid layouts as "pre-writing" exercises for these additional essays.

2   Twentieth century events have profoundly altered the lives of people in the underdeveloped regions of the globe.

20th Century Events

Urban growth in Latin America
Tribal warfare in Nigeria
Religious differences in India
Vietnam War
Communist victory in the Chinese Civil War
Lebanese Civil War
Creation of Israel

Select *three* of the above events. For *each* one, describe how the event created a problem of political or economic refugees. [5,5,5]

3   Adjustment of immigrants and migrants in new lands is often difficult and sometimes painful.

   a   Describe *one* problem which makes settlement in a new country difficult for refugees. [3]

   b   Choose *three* of the countries listed below. For *each* one, describe a specific economic or political circumstance which caused large numbers of people to leave the country at that time. [3,3,3]

Countries

17th and 18th Century - England
19th Century - China
Mid-19th Century - Ireland
Late 19th Century - Italy
Post World War II - Mexico
Post World War I - Soviet Union

   c   Describe how a *specific* country has benefited from the settlement of large numbers of people from other lands. [3]

LESSON 5

Economic Growth and Development

World Trade and Finance

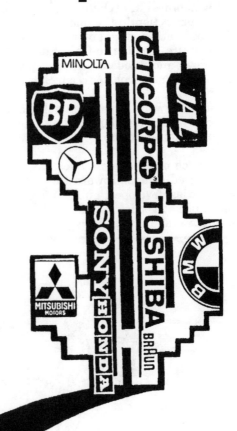

World
Issue   1

Feudalism

The chaos and disorder in Europe that resulted from the fall of the vast Roman Empire (476 A.D.) led to the development of **feudalism** and **manorialism**. Similar systems also developed in Japan and lasted several centuries longer than they did in Europe.

A **feudal overlord** (supreme regional noble) provided a **vassal** (lesser noble sworn to serve the overlord) with a **fief** (share of land), protection, and justice. In exchange, a vassal had to provide military service, feudal dues, and duty at the overlord's court.

The vassal's landholding (a **fief** granted by an overlord) was the basis for a traditional economic system called **manorialism**. On the vassal's manor, farmers and laborers called **serfs** were legally bound to live and work the lord's lands. Serfs provided the lord with produce from the parts of the land they were assigned. They also gave him part of what they produced using his mill and winepress. In exchange, the lord provided them with land to work, justice, and protection in the manor house's fortress during attacks. It was a primitive and rather stagnant way of life. It was barely more than subsistence agriculture. The **three-field horticultural system** (two worked while one lay fallow) and wooden tools kept production low and scarcity was commonplace. Since no surpluses occurred, trade was nearly nonexistent.

While manors were largely self-sufficient economic entities, the system of exchanged loyalties and landholding under feudalism created military and political **interdependence**.

During much of the Middle Ages, disorder made it necessary for the manors to be armed camps. Toward the end of the period, change occurred. As towns and cities developed, guilds of craftsmen and merchants began to produce and market goods. Interdependent relationships began to develop between the rural and urban areas.

Commercial Revolution

and the Rise
of Capitalism

Crusades
↓
Age of Exploration
↓
Comm. Rev.
↓
Capitalism
↓
Command Sys.
↳ *(Ripps)*
↳ *Mercam*

Continued change and the introduction of new cultural ideas brought back by the **Crusaders** led to greater demand for products from the Middle and Far East. The resulting **Age of Exploration** and the **Commercial Revolution** brought economic growth and the beginning of world trade. The increased demand led to the use of the **domestic system** (also called the putting out system) of production, banking, and insurance. **Capitalism** (free market economy) began to evolve as an economic system. It provided for private property and profit and allowed the entrepreneur considerable freedom of enterprise.

Indust. Rev.
1750

The absolute monarchies of the 16th-18th centuries interfered with the freedom by imposing a command system called mercantilism as their economic policy. The goal of **mercantilism** was to increase the nation's supply of gold and silver by the use of colonies, tariffs, quotas, subsidies, and other devices designed to promote self-sufficiency and a favorable balance of trade.

The Industrial Revolution and
the Development
of Socialism

The continued demand for larger quantities of goods led to the Industrial Revolution. It began about 1750 in England. Technological developments in the textile industry (flying shuttle, spinning jenny, power loom, etc.) tremendously increased production. The invention of Watt's steam engine moved production into centralized factories.

As industrialization progressed, labor conditions in factories and mines became brutal. Exploitation of workers eventually led to reform laws and the development of **socialism**. Socialism places limits on capitalism's private ownership and advocates a high degree of public ownership of the means of production. In the mid-19th century, socialist extremists **Karl Marx** and **Friedrich Engels** wrote the *Communist Manifesto*. It called for the violent overthrow of the **capitalist class** (owners of industry) by the united **proletariat** (industrial working class) and the creation of a whole new economic and political system run by workers for workers. The book became the philosophical basis for later communist movements.

The Industrial Revolution spread rapidly in Western Europe and the United States in the last part of the 19th century. However, the most rapid industrial progress was achieved in countries such as Japan after the Meiji Restoration and the Soviet Union after the Russian Revolution of 1917. It has only been in recent years, however, that massive industrial growth has raised widespread environmental concerns. Pollution of rivers such as the Rhine and Thames, problems of acid rain, and the **Greenhouse Effect** are reminders of the fragile nature of the environment (see the section on Environmental Concerns).

World Issue

Modern Trends in Economic Development

Since the end of World War II in 1945, there have been a number of distinctive trends in economic development, world trade, and finance. Much attention has focused on Third World countries. These countries have struggled to make the choice between **capitalism** (market structure) and **socialism/communism** (command structure). Most of these countries have chosen **mixed systems** containing private enterprise but reserving a large role for central planning. These countries lack middle class know-how and development capital.

Developing countries face a constant struggle between the need to reinvest capital and the need to spend to provide for consumers' wants. This has led countries such as Argentina, Mexico, Brazil, Nigeria, and the Ivory Coast to borrow large sums from foreign banks, foreign governments, and international organizations (World Bank, International Monetary Fund). These debtor nations now face potential bankruptcy because they lack the resources to repay the loans. They continue to be exporters of lower cost raw materials and importers of higher cost finished

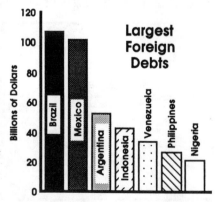

Largest Foreign Debts

products. As interdependence grows in the modern world, **economic equity** (fairness) in the division of the world's scarce resources has become a persistent global issue.

Another interdependency trend has been toward regional economic cooperation or unity. An outstanding example is the **Common Market** (European Economic Community) which plans a united marketplace for Western Europe in 1992. The **Latin American Trade Association**, and the **Central American Common Market** are other regional examples.

The opening of the Berlin Wall and the reunification of Germany in the late 1980's illustrate the sweep of recent developments in Eastern Europe and the independent republics of the former U.S.S.R. The cautiousness of former Soviet President **Mikhail Gorbachev** toward the perestroika reforms he triggered in the late 1980's was a major problem. Reactionary Politboro leaders attempted an anti-reform coup against Gorbachev in the summer of 1991. But, democratic resistance rallied around the Russian Federation's President **Boris Yeltsin**. The Red Army refused the coup leaders' orders to fire on civilians. The coup disintegrated and so did the Soviet Union.

The former Soviet republics declared independence. Yeltsin emerged as a primary leader. He negotiated an end to the Soviet Union and created a loose military and economic alliance (Commonwealth of Independent States). Gorbachev resigned as President and the country that Lenin created in 1917 was no more.

Most of the former communist countries in Eastern Europe and Central Asia are attempting to move their economies toward market systems. Leaders such as Yeltsin and Lech Walesa of Poland have taken dramatic and painful steps toward market economies. In Romania, Bulgaria, and Kazakhstan, leaders are maintaining socialist approaches.

Increasing interdependence among nations, along with the blinding speed of technological change, especially in the computer and scientific fields, have also had a great impact on economic growth and world trade relationships.

Gorbachev's attempts to hold the former U.S.S.R. together failed in 1991 when most of the Soviet republics declared independence.

Additional Information on Growth and Development and World Trade

This is a very broad topic. Consult your text on economic development and economic systems. In *N&N's Global Studies Review Text,* more information on can be found in each Unit, Sub-Section IV and on

Africa   [pgs. 24-26, 28, 37-38, 42-46, 65, 72, 81-84]
South and Southeast Asia   [pgs. 102-103, 109-111, 114-116]
China   [pgs. 129-130, 133-137, 144-146];
Japan   [pgs. 163-165, 176-179]
Latin America   [pgs. 205-206, 218-220, 224-225];
Middle East   [pgs. 238-239, 250-252, 258-262, 282-286]
Western Europe   [pgs. 307-308, 311-313, 320-322, 335-338]
Soviet Union and Eastern Europe   [pgs. 348-361]
World Today   [pgs. 348, 350, 357-360]

Questions

Base your answer to question 1 on the chart below and on your knowledge of social studies.

Debtor Nations and Debt Amounts			
Nation	*1984 Debt (in billions)*	*1988 Debt (in billions)*	*Debt per capita (in thousands)*
Argentina	59.6	43.6	1,863
Brazil	120.1	91.9	840
Mexico	107.4	86.1	1,310
Poland	39.1	26.5	1,029
Nigeria	30.5	12.9	285
Philippines	30.2	24.3	517

1   Although Argentina has a smaller total debt than Brazil in 1988 and 1984, it has a larger per capita debt because it has
   1   borrowed more money from foreign governments
   2   a smaller population
   3   less ability to repay the debt
   4   a more favorable balance of trade

2   A major reason for high debt levels among developing countries is their
   1   need for investment capital
   2   increasing social security costs for an aging population
   3   decreasing reliance on raw material exports
   4   refusal to adopt new farming methods

3   Which conclusion is correct?
   1   Third World debt is a world wide problem.
   2   Only oil producing countries have high debts.
   3   Communist countries do not have debts.
   4   The highest debts are in African countries.

4   The Middle Ages in Western Europe was characterized by
      1   the manor system and the importance of land ownership
      2   absolute monarchies and strong central governments
      3   decreased emphasis on religion in daily life
      4   extensive trade with Asia and the Middle East

5   The European Economic Community was formed primarily because there was
      1   a desire to maintain the military balance of power in Europe
      2   a desire by European nations to counteract the political influence of the United States in the world
      3   pressure by the United States to eliminate all trade barriers
      4   a growing recognition by European leaders that their nations share common problems

6   The invention of spinning and weaving machinery increased the number of workers in the textile industry in Europe because
      1   the early textile machines could not produce goods as efficiently as hand labor
      2   laws prohibited women and children from working with machinery
      3   the demand for goods increased as goods became cheaper to produce
      4   the unions required that more workers be hired to maintain the machines

7   The main features of a capitalistic economic system are
      1   powerful labor unions and fixed prices
      2   export quotas and state ownership of basic industries
      3   private ownership and the profit motive
      4   central planning by government and full employment

8   Which was a result of the Commercial Revolution?
      1   decline in population growth in Europe
      2   shift of power from western Europe to eastern Europe
      3   spread of feudalism throughout western Europe
      4   expansion of European influence overseas

9   A main idea of Karl Marx and Friedrich Engels' *Communist Manifesto* is that the proletariat
      1   would need foreign help to achieve its revolutionary ends
      2   had to cooperate with the capitalists to gain economic rewards
      3   should allow the capitalists to control the means of production
      4   must unite to overthrow the capitalist class

10   Which is characteristic of a feudal society?
      1   rapid social change
      2   high literacy rate
      3   industrial-based economy
      4   rigid class structure

11   A major problem for many Latin American countries has been the
      1   payment of their debts to foreign countries
      2   shortage of water
      3   rapidly decreasing population
      4   shortage of labor in agricultural areas

12   "The average worker can never obtain more than a minimum level of living. The worker is deprived of the wealth he himself has created. The state is a committee of the bourgeoisie for the exploitation of the people." The ideas in the quotation would most likely be expressed by a
1   Christian Humanist
2   mercantilist
3   laissez-faire capitalist
4   Marxist socialist

Model Essay

1   Change is a constant feature in the world economy.

Time Periods

Middle Ages
Commercial Revolution
Industrial Revolution
Post World War II

Select *three* of the time periods below and for *each* one selected:

- Describe *two* economic changes that occurred.

- Discuss *two* results of the changes. [5,5,5]

Pre-writing Strategy: Before you begin to write your answer in full sentences, lay out your preliminary information on the lines and grid below and on the next page. Be certain that you know *two* changes and a result of each change for each time period selected. Discuss *each* of the time periods in a separate paragraph. Also, remember that to prove a change occurred, you *must* describe the original condition.

Time Period: Commercial Revolution	
Economic Changes:	*Results of the Changes:*

Time Period: Industrial Revolution	
Economic Changes: Production changed from the domestic (putting out) system to the factory system. Government economic policy changed from mercantilism to the laissez-faire market idea of Adam Smith. Smith's market system encouraged investment and expansion of the production.	*Results of the Changes:*

Time Period: Post World War II Era	
Economic Changes: The predominance of economic power has shifted from Europe to the U.S. and Japan. Also, the world has become increasingly interdependent.	*Results of the Changes:*

   After completing the grid, write out your answers in three separate paragraphs, using complete sentences.

Additional Practice Essays

It is suggested that you design and complete your own grid layouts as "pre-writing" exercises for these additional essays.

2 In the 20th century, technological developments have had both positive and negative effects.

Technological Developments

Space technology
Nuclear energy
Computer revolution
Advanced medical techniques
Green revolution
Internal combustion engine

Choose *three* technological developments from the list above. For *each* technological development chosen, discuss *one* positive effect and *one* negative effect of the technological development on 20th century society. In your answer, include one specific example of each technological development. [5,5,5]

3 Throughout history, there has been a strong interrelationship between economic circumstances and political structures.

Economic Circumstances / Political Structures

Exploitation of Industrial Workers – Rise of Marxist Socialism
Growth of Commercial Towns – Capitalism
Common Market – Interdependence
Mercantilism – Colonial Empires
Lack of Resources - Third World Command Systems

Select *three* of the above pairs of economic circumstances and political structures. For *each* one selected:

- Discuss a *specific* time period and nation where an example of this combination of economic circumstance and political structure occurred.

- Explain the relationship of the economic circumstance to the political structure. [5,5,5]

LESSON 6

Preserving the Environment vs. Energy Needs

Throughout history, the people of the Earth have behaved as if there were infinite amounts of air, soil, water, and other natural resources. The result has often been shocking. Portions of the environment have been gradually devastated. Humankind's survival depends on the protective **biosphere** (protective layer of air, soil, and water surrounding it). A balance must be achieved between developmental growth and preservation of the environment.

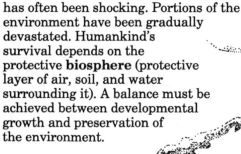

In this section, there are four case studies: **Desertification, Deforestation, Urban-Industrial Pollution,** and **Oil and Alternative Energy Sources.** In each, the focus is on the critical concepts of choice, interdependence, technology, and change.

Desertification

Drought and famine have always been serious problems threatening human existence. The twin threat can be seen today in Africa, where in the late 1980's the Sahara desert grew an estimated six miles wider per year.

In an area called the "Sahel" in West Africa, the process of **desertification** (loss of available land to the desert) has occurred because of soil erosion. This, combined with severe drought in Mauritania, Mali, Niger, and Chad, brought widespread starvation and death to the region's people and herds.

The disaster was not entirely created by nature. The region's farmers and nomads have over-cut trees for firewood. They maintained large goat, camel, sheep, and cattle herds which overgrazed the limited grasslands. In addition, they over-cultivated the land. These practices pushed the local ecological balance beyond its limits. The resulting desertification has created a land not suitable for human life.

Of all the causes of desertification, overgrazing by the herds of nomadic tribes appears to have done the most extensive damage. Because they lose so many of their animals to drought, herders intentionally increase the size of their herds to compensate for the losses. Of course this only compounds the problem, but they hope that by raising more in good years, they will have milk and meat to survive in bad years. The additional grazing of the over-large herds prevents the land from regenerating its vegetation, and the land becomes increasingly barren.

As nomads move on, they continue to cut what little wood remains, robbing the soil of its "tree holding power" (anchorage) it might have, and erosion becomes worse.

The solution would involve a cooperative international effort of severe governmental action which would interfere with the traditional nomadic lifestyle of desert dwellers. African leaders would have to adopt a program to settle the various ethnic groups in definite areas.

The United Nations has offered educational and technical assistance to teach the groups conservation and land management. But, achieving such a major change will be difficult.

Deforestation

Another devastating act that contributes significantly to soil erosion is **deforestation** (the over-cutting of timber resources for commercial purposes). The World Resources Institute, the World Bank, and the International Monetary Fund have jointly stated that for every ten trees cut in the tropics, only one is replaced. Conservationists say this carelessness affects the ecology of nearly 74,000 acres a day in Brazil's Amazon rain forests. At this rate, the present generation will strip nearly a million square miles of Amazon Basin land area.

Without commercial reforestation, the thin layer of topsoil that remains after cutting down the trees is exposed to heavy rains and becomes eroded. The process of desertification begins.

Landless peasants compound the problem by settling in the rain-forest and clearing the land in "slash and burn" fashion. The land quickly wears out, and the farmers move on. Inadequate land management eventually exposes the rain-forest land to the same forces of erosion mentioned above.

Cattle ranchers often move onto land abandoned by peasants, but the grasses that grow on the cleared rain-forest land are not meant for cattle grazing, and the ranches are abandoned.

When the ecological balance is over-strained, the land often becomes unsuitable for human habitation. The quality of life is adversely affected.

The destruction is not just limited to Brazil, it is global in scope. Tropical rain-forests in Indonesia, Thailand, Ghana, the Ivory Coast, and Ecuador have also been devastated by this careless development.

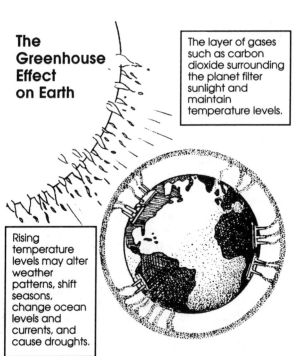

The Greenhouse Effect on Earth

The layer of gases such as carbon dioxide surrounding the planet filter sunlight and maintain temperature levels.

Rising temperature levels may alter weather patterns, shift seasons, change ocean levels and currents, and cause droughts.

Deforestation, modern industries, and urbanized life produce too many waste gases that have radically altered the composition of the planet's protective atmosphere.

The current debate over the **"Greenhouse Effect"** indicates that there are global consequences resulting from deforestation (see illustration on the previous page). Preservation of the world's rain-forests is now seen as critical to insuring the climatic stability of the Earth.

As with most environmental problems, solutions carry high economic costs and painful choices. Since the lumber is a major export for many tropical countries, developed nations must help offset the cost of controlling commercial lumbering. International authorities, such as the **World Resources Institute** recommend banks be monitored so that capital would only be invested in sound forestry operations. Banks could also promote forgiveness of foreign debts for conservation programs monitored by the World Bank or a global environmental trust fund.

Urban Industrial Pollution (Acid Rain)

Massive traffic jams, ugly factories, garbage and sewage problems, and a lack of **green space** (parks and gardens) characterize many of the world's urban centers. In many of the developing nations, unmanaged **urban growth**, has caused severe ecological damage in the breakdown of air and water quality and **traffic pollution** (noise and air). Western European nations share all of these problems. Recently, the twelve nations of the European Community launched an environmental campaign to combat pollution. Now, countries in violation of its environmental codes can be brought before the European Court of Justice.

Often, one country's industries severely impact the environment of its neighbors. **Acid rain** (air pollutants that travel in precipitation) has become a global concern. Natural resources such as lakes, forests, plant and animal life suffer the adverse effects of acid rain pollution. Even our great landmarks to the past in the form of sculptures and historic buildings suffer from the corrosion caused by this form of contamination.

Acid rain scars marble and corrodes bronze destroying art as well as life. This has forced cultural as well as environmental groups to join forces and promote legislation to prevent the burning of sulfuric coal which is estimated to cause over 80% of the pollutants in acid rain.

Scientists observe that acid rain deposits have killed the fish and plant life of nearly 20% of the lakes of Norway and Sweden. Scandinavian biologists have pumped lime into many lakes to lower the effect of the acid on the remaining fish, but the only realistic answer is to reduce the levels of sulfur and nitrogen oxides. This can only be done by national and international pollution actions.

However, many of the world's political and industrial leaders feel environmental protection interferes with economic growth. In many countries, such leaders have combined to defeat protective legislation and treaty agreements.

Failure to act decisively has caused unnecessary human suffering (lung disease) and billions of dollars in often irreparable damages to irreplaceable physical resources.

A new attitude has to emerge for humankind to have a more harmonious relationship to exist with nature. Recognizing which resources are finite and considering long-range goals can help insure human survival. Protecting our biosphere means creatively modifying and using nature in a productive, yet protective, way. Ultimately, an attitude of stewardship among all nations must occur to maintain a continued supply of raw materials and a clean environment.

Oil and Alternate Energy Resources

The ideal energy source is one that is plentiful, renewable, clean, efficient, and inexpensive. It is a basic truth that, at present, such a source does not exist. The industrially developed nations, which consume enormous amounts of energy, have long relied on petroleum without regard to its conservation or its affects on pollution of the environment. As long as petroleum was plentiful and cheap, the harmful side effects of its use were often overlooked.

The situation changed rather abruptly in the last generation when oil producing nations organized the **OPEC cartel** (Organization of Petroleum Exporting Countries). Through joint economic and political action, OPEC nations raised crude oil prices. During the 1973 Arab-Israeli war, an embargo was placed on shipments of oil to those nations which supported Israel. As supplies began to dwindle, shortages forced up the price of oil. By 1979, prices had quadrupled. Fabulous wealth came to the oil-rich Arab nations, but it caused severe inflation throughout the rest of the world. Conservation became the theme for world consumers. A trend developed for energy efficient automobiles, homes, and appliances.

Western nations also sought alternative energy sources. Nuclear, solar, wind, natural gas, and hydro-energy sources, once considered too expensive, began to look more reasonable as oil prices rose.

By the 1980's, these measures reduced some of the dependence on Mid-East oil. As demand for oil decreased, an oversupply developed which forced severe budgetary cuts among the OPEC nations. The non-oil producing Muslim nations of the Middle East suffered because they had grown extremely dependent on their oil rich neighbors for financial aid and employment for their people. Arab oil money, which had previously been invested in foreign countries and loaned to foreign governments and corporations, was restricted. Oversupply caused oil prices to decline, but they have recently begun to rise again as complacent Western nations seem to be tiring of conservation.

The case of oil indicates the interdependence of nations. It shows how their economic and political fates are intertwined with finite resources. It underscores the need for cooperation, conservation, and joint research to seek renewable energy sources.

Additional Information on Environment/Energy

Consult your text on scarcity, pollution, and environmental problems in the various regions. In *N&N's Global Studies Review Text*, more information on can be found on

Environmental issues in Europe [pg. 278]
Environmental issues in today's world [pg. 353]
Energy resources in today's world [pg. 351]

Questions

1   Many global issues such as overcrowding and pollution of the
    environment are a direct result of
    1   high unemployment
    2   overpopulation
    3   a farm based economy
    4   a balance of World Trade

2   OPEC is a group of nations that formed an agreement to control
    1   environmental pollution
    2   overpopulation in underdeveloped regions
    3   financial rewards for environmental conservation
    4   the quantity and price of petroleum

*Base your answer to question 3 on the chart below and your knowledge of
social studies.*

Oil Production in Sample Countries			
Country	**Reserves (in barrels)**	**Production (in barrels)**	**Years Reserves Will Last**
Algeria	8,200,000	293,095	28
Egypt	3,000,000	218,270	14
Kuwait	64,900,000	346,655	188
Libya	23,000,000	415,000	55
Saudi Arabia	165,000,000	3,500,000	47
United Arab Emirates	30,000,000	550,000	55

3   Which nation had the greatest oil reserves in 1981?
    1   Saudi Arabia
    2   Egypt
    3   Libya
    4   Kuwait

4   A major world region where desertification has recently caused
    widespread famine and death has been
    1   China's Gobi Desert
    2   Africa's Sahel
    3   India's Punjab
    4   Brazil's Amazon Basin

5   Desertification is caused by
    1   flooding of low lying plains
    2   overgrazing
    3   strip mining
    4   overpopulation

6   Widespread deforestation of the tropical rain-forests is linked to the changing of
1   ocean life
2   climatic patterns
3   traditional family lifestyles
4   alternative energy sources

7   Which region has currently organized international sanctions against environmental pollution?
1   Western Europe
2   Western Africa
3   The Middle East
4   Southeast Asia

8   A major contributor to the creation of acid rain has been the
1   underground nuclear testing
2   burning of sulfuric coal
3   emissions control testing of nations
4   wood burning stoves

Model Essay

(Note: Most often, environmental/energy problems are included as one of the choices in questions on world problems.)

1   Humankind's survival depends on the protective biosphere (protective layer of air, soil, and water surrounding the Earth). A balance must be achieved between developmental growth and preservation of the environment.

Environmental Situations

Deforestation of Brazil's Amazon Basin rain forest
Desertification of Africa's Sahel
Destruction of Scandinavian lakes from British Industrial Acid Rain
OPEC's control of Petroleum supplies in 1970's

a   Select *two* of the above environmental situations. For *each* one chosen, explain a problem connected with the situation. [5,5]

b   For *one* of the situations discussed in part *a*, indicate a way people are seeking to resolve the problem. [5]

Pre-writing Strategy: Before you begin to write your answer in full sentences, lay out your preliminary information on the grids on the next page to be sure that you have all the required parts of the answer.

a) Environmental Situations	
Environmental Situations: Desertification of Africa's Sahel	Problem:
Deforestation of Brazil's Amazon Basin rain forest	

b) Seeking to Solve the Environmental Problem

Solution:

Problem of deforestation is global since lumber is a major export for many tropical countries, such as Brazil. Developed nations must help by offsetting the cost of controlling of commercial lumbering in the Amazon.

Additional Practice Essay

It is suggested that you design and complete your own grid layout as a "pre-writing" exercise for this additional essay.

2   The world has great problems with its viable energy producing resources.

Viable Energy Resources

Nuclear power
Hydroelectric power
Wind power
Solar power
Wood power

Select any *three* of the energy resources listed above and describe the advantages and disadvantages of their use. [5,5,5]

LESSON 7
Human Rights

Human rights are the natural rights to which all human beings are universally entitled. Just and fair claims to natural, traditional, legal powers and privileges have been voiced since the beginning of time. Ancient Greek philosophy, Christian metaphysics, and Enlightenment writings discussed such principles. Examples of these rights include freedoms of speech, assembly, worship, and the right to the dignity of a decent standard of living.

In the modern era, America's *Declaration of Independence* (1776) and France's *Declaration of the Rights of Man* (1789) proclaimed the universal desire for natural rights and for equality. In 1948, **Eleanor Roosevelt** oversaw the writing and adoption of the United Nations' *Universal Declaration of Human Rights*. It said that all individuals should be able to live their lives with true dignity free from oppression and discrimination. It condemned the inequality and injustice of totalitarian governments and made their eradication a goal for all humans.

History and current events teach us that few societies devote themselves to preserving human rights. The denial of the sanctity of human life in totalitarian regimes such as Nazi Germany, South Africa, and Red China are clear examples. In Latin America, brutal treatment of dissenters in Chile, Cuba, Nicaragua, and El Salvador remind us we should never take our rights for granted.

World
Issue

The Holocaust: Nazi Genocide Against the Jews

Jews experienced persecution in Germany, Eastern Europe, Austria-Hungary, and Russia for a long time. In Germany, the mistreatment intensified when the Nazis came to power in 1933. Jews were denied civil service and teaching positions and the right to own businesses. Jews were deemed political threats to Hitler's regime. They lost their citizenship and the right to marry under the anti-semitic **Nuremburg Laws** of 1935. Gradually, they were forced into labor camps such as the one at Dachau.

As the Nazis conquered Poland and other Eastern European states, this treatment was extended to Jews living there. During World War II, Hitler's "Final Solution" was to convert the concentration camps to death camps where approximately six million Jews were starved, gassed, or shot to death in places such as Auschwitz and Treblinka.

The Nazis conducted a program of **genocide** (systematic extermination of a race of people) against the Jews. This program has become known as **"The Holocaust."** Not until the Allied forces liberated the concentration camps in 1945 was the world truly aware of the extent of this insanity.

The world reeled at the shocking evidence exposed as the Nuremburg war crime trials of 1946 revealed the genocide to be the most heinous crime ever committed against any group of people.

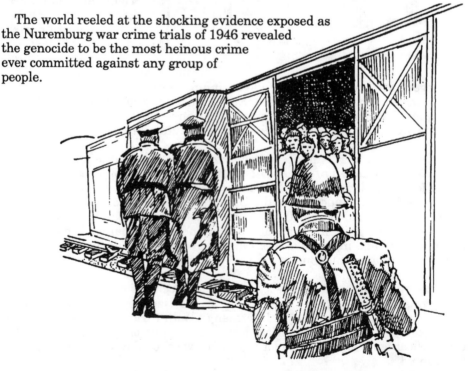

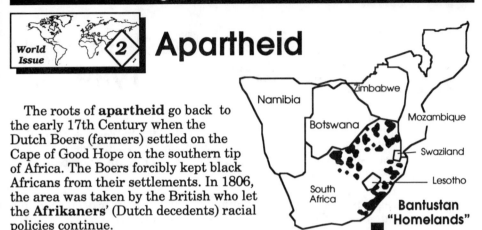

Apartheid

The roots of **apartheid** go back to the early 17th Century when the Dutch Boers (farmers) settled on the Cape of Good Hope on the southern tip of Africa. The Boers forcibly kept black Africans from their settlements. In 1806, the area was taken by the British who let the **Afrikaners'** (Dutch decedents) racial policies continue.

Apartheid segregation policies were strengthened when the British unified their South African colonies as the Union of South Africa just before World War I. The **Native Lands Act of 1913** and the **Group Areas Act of 1950** insured power for the white only groups running the government. These laws restricted black Africans to certain "homeland" areas, imposed a pass system of work permits, and restricted travel and movement in other ways.

Resisting calls for human rights and equality, the white minority passed a constitution in 1984 under which 73% of the nation's population were denied the right to vote.

The South African government was condemned by the United Nations and even the International Olympic Committee for its denial of human rights. International trade sanctions were levied by governments and private multinational corporations. Anti-apartheid leaders such as Nobel Peace Prize winner **Bishop Desmond Tutu** and **Nelson Mandela** tried to intensify global pressure on the government. They staged boycotts and demonstrations. In the 1990's, President **F. W. De Klerk**'s moderate party shows a willingness to reform racial policy. They were encouraged by a 1992 national referendum in which 68% of the white voters agreed to abolish apartheid.

**The Imbalance Between "White" And "Black" Representation
In South Africa**

Chinese Student Rebellion of 1989

In the Spring of 1989, thousands of Chinese students began to demonstrate against corruption in Beijing and Shanghai. The demonstrations spread to most of China's major cities. Student leaders began to criticize the slow pace of reform in government and called for greater economic and personal freedoms for the Chinese people.

Such a courageous public outcry for human rights had never been seen in a totalitarian state before. World media began to focus attention on the student demonstrators in Beijing's **Ti'ananmen Square**.

At first, the communist government allowed the dissent hoping it would die down. As the movement gained momentum, a power struggle erupted inside the ruling Communist Party's Central Committee. The more liberal party leader, **Zhao Ziyang**, was forced out by conservative communist hard-liners led by Premier **Li Peng** and the new party secretary, **Jiang Zemin**.

On June 4th, the hard-liners convinced aging paramount leader, **Deng Xiaopong**, to unleash a brutal Red Army attack to crush the students before a watching world. Typical of a totalitarian state, the communist government denied any repression, but estimates of the Ti'ananmen deaths and later arrests and executions exceeded five thousand.

A Chinese student stands peacefully, blocking the advance of a Red Army tank.

Additional Information on World Issue Refugees

Consult your text on human rights. In *N&N's Global Studies Review Text,* more information on can be found on

Spanish encomiendas in Latin America [pg. 177]
Untouchables in India [pgs. 60 and 177]
Uganda under Idi Amin [pg. 356]
Slavery [pgs. 24-25]
Solidarity in Poland [pg. 342]
Stalin's purges in the 1930's [pgs. 321-322]
Hungarian Revolution [pg. 331]
Czechoslovakian Revolution [pg. 331]
The World Today [pgs. 356-357]

Questions

Base your answer to questions 1 and 2 on the cartoon at the right and on your knowledge of social studies.

"Witnesses for the Prosecution"

1   The cartoon is primarily concerned with determining responsibility for which situation?
   1   use of poison gas during World War I
   2   slave labor camps in the Soviet Union during the Stalin era
   3   the holocaust in Europe during the 1930's and 1940's
   4   current apartheid practices in the Republic of South Africa

2   The trial symbolized in the cartoon is significant because it was the first time that
   1   the United Nations International Court of Justice worked effectively
   2   individuals were prosecuted for crimes against humanity
   3   war guilt was applied to a whole nation
   4   international law was enforced

3   Which is a basic belief shared by all totalitarian regimes?
     1   Written constitutions and elections are necessary.
     2   Hostile neighbors may be ignored.
     3   Human rights are less important than the requirements of the state.
     4   Membership in peace-keeping organizations is vital.

Base your answer to question 4 on the cartoon at the right and on your knowledge of social studies.

4   Which statement best expresses the main point of the cartoon?
     1   Eastern European courtship practices are like those in democratic countries.
     2   The NATO Alliance is blocking reform in Eastern Europe.
     3   Reform movements have begun to change Eastern Europe.
     4   Democracy is a fading dream in communist states.

The passage below is an excerpt from the Nuremburg Laws of 1935. Base your answer to questions 5 and 6 on the excerpt and your knowledge of social studies.

Reich Citizenship Law and Decree
Only such persons as are of German or kindred stock and who have proved by their conduct that they are willing and fit loyally to serve the German people and Reich are citizens ... Reich citizens shall be the sole possessors of complete political rights.

5   The law in the excerpt was designed to
     1   protect the rights of German minorities
     2   extend citizenship to all people living in Germany
     3   put racist theories into public policies
     4   insure political freedom

6   The Nuremburg Laws were partially responsible for
     1   the occurrence of the Holocaust
     2   the extension of citizenship to minority group members
     3   the creation of a classless society in Germany
     4   increased nationalism for minorities living in Germany

7   Human rights and self determination were principles proclaimed after
     World War II by
     1   the French colonial rulers
     2   a United Nations declaration
     3   the Nazi Party
     4   the white leaders of South Africa

*Base your answer to questions 8 and 9 on the passage below and on your
knowledge of social studies.*

> Josef Stalin was one of Lenin's chief assistants. After Lenin's death,
> Stalin eliminated his opponents and became leader of his country. He set
> up a totalitarian state. Peasants were forced to join collective farms.
> Those who objected were starved, shot, or sent to forced labor camps.
> Hundreds of thousands died during these years. Stalin also put strict
> controls on the society. Even scientists who did not agree with theories
> accepted by the state lost their jobs.

8   This passage describes life during the
     1   Boxer Rebellion of 1900
     2   Cultural Revolution of 1968
     3   the 1920–1940 period in the Soviet Union
     4   Chinese Student Rebellion of 1989

9   Which statement best describes the main idea of the passage?
     1   Stalin was one of Lenin's chief assistants.
     2   Stalin was a ruthless dictator.
     3   Many people have died in the 20th Century.
     4   Scientists lose their jobs during a totalitarian regime.

*Base your answer to
question 10 on the cartoon
at the right and on your
knowledge of social
studies.*

10   Which of the
     following offers the
     best explanation for
     the cartoon at the
     right?

     1   Leaders of foreign nations are always less truthful than American
          presidents.
     2   Totalitarian leaders put state concerns above human rights.
     3   Women rulers tend to be more sympathetic to human rights than
          male leaders.
     4   The philosophy of "the end justifies the means" did not survive into
          the 20th Century.

Model Essay

1   Human rights of certain groups of people have been violated through official governmental policy and/or by traditional social patterns.

Groups

Blacks in South Africa
Untouchables in India
Inhabitants of Kampuchea (Cambodia)
Jews in Europe
Palestinian refugees in the Middle East

Choose *three* of the groups from the list above. For *each* one chosen:

• Describe a *specific* violation of human rights that the group suffered or is suffering.

• Describe efforts that were made or are being made to overcome or compensate for violations of that group's human rights.   [5,5,5]

Pre-writing Strategy: Before writing your answer in sentences, lay out preliminary information on the grid format below and on the next page.

Group: Blacks in South Africa	
Violation of Rights:	*Restoration of Rights:*

Group: Untouchables in India	
Violation of Rights:	*Restoration of Rights:*

Group: Jews in Europe	
Violation of Rights:	*Restoration of Rights:*
Long history of discrimination and violent treatment because of religious and cultural differences. Nazi genocide executed six million Jews.	

After completing the grid, write out your answers in three separate paragraphs, using complete sentences.

Additional Practice Essays

It is suggested that you design and complete your own grid layouts as "pre-writing" exercises for these additional essays.

2　In 1948, the General Assembly of the United Nations approved the Convention on the Prevention and Punishment of the Crime of Genocide, declaring that any act intended to destroy, in whole or in part, a national, ethnic, racial, or religious group was to be considered "a crime against humanity."

Identify *three* groups which have been victims of attempted genocide, as defined above. For *each* group, discuss the time, place, circumstances, and justification used by those attempting genocide, and the results of the attempt. [5,5,5]

3　Throughout history, many groups have experienced denials of human rights through discrimination.

Methods of Discrimination

unfair taxation
forced abandonment of culture
denial of education
denial of political rights
denial of natural and civil rights
imprisonment and/or execution

Select *three* of the methods listed above. Use a *different* group for each method selected For *each* action:

- Describe a specific example of its use against a particular group. (Be sure to include the place, time, circumstances in your example.)

- Discuss a significant effect of this method of discrimination on the group. [5,5,5]

LESSON 8 Determination of Political and Economic Systems

There has always been great diversity among the political and economic systems found in the world. Each nation adopts (and adapts) systems which best fit its culture, its current conditions, and its goals for the future.

Sometimes, nations will blend two systems. For example, Great Britain is a parliamentary democracy and constitutional monarchy. Frequently, nations change or adjust (amend) these systems as conditions change. Sometimes major change occurs slowly, through evolution, as was the case with Britain. Sometimes, major political changes occur rapidly, by revolution, as in countries such as France, Cuba, and Russia.

Political change is often accompanied by alterations in the economic system. The resulting variations on basic structures are numerous. Although societies based on a political / economic system such as democracy and capitalism have certain characteristics in common, there are usually considerable differences from country to country.

Political Systems

The three most basic types of political systems are democracy, monarchy, and totalitarianism. One basis for comparing their characteristics is seeing who makes the key decisions in the society.

Democracy

Political systems based on **democracy** involve a high degree of decision making by citizens. Citizenship in a democracy also involves considerable responsibilities. For example, citizens are expected to obey the laws, vote, serve on juries, and if necessary, serve in the military.

Democratic systems strive to protect people's **natural rights** (such as life, liberty, property, and pursuit of happiness). They also protect citizens' **civil rights** (such as the freedoms of speech, press, religion, assembly) which are extensions of basic natural rights.

Democracies strive to provide for a rule of law that maintains an equitable administration of justice and elections that are fair and offer a choice of candidates. The most basic premise of democratic government is that it exists to serve the interests of its citizens.

Examples of democratic political structures include:

- **Direct** (pure) **democracy** involves citizens directly in the lawmaking process. Ancient Athens practiced direct democracy. Adult male citizens were expected to go to the Assembly to help make the laws. Town meetings in the early United States also used direct democracy.

- **Representative democracy** (republic) involves citizens electing people to represent them in the legislative, executive, and, sometimes in the judicial processes of government. This is more common today than direct democracy because of the scope of modern governmental activities and the number of people involved.

  The United States Congress is a form of representative democracy. The U.S. chief executive is elected by an even more indirect system: the people choose special electors (Electoral College) who cast official ballots for President and Vice-President.

- **Parliamentary democracy** also involves the election of representatives, but generally, the chief executive (Prime Minister) is selected by the majority party in the lower house of the legislature. The government of Great Britain is a parliamentary democracy headed by a constitutional monarch.

Monarchy

In a **monarchy**, decision making is in the hands of a hereditary ruler whose title might be king, prince, emperor, or tsar. There are many different types of monarchies. In some cases, the monarch (ruler) has almost complete power, in other instances, the monarch's power may be limited by a constitution giving other bodies power.

There are only a few monarchies left today, but prior to World War I, some of the most powerful countries in the world were monarchies.

Peter The Great

Examples of monarchic political structures include:

- **Absolute monarchy**, in which the ruler has almost total decision making power. The monarch can tax, make laws, appoint government officials, and declare war without the approval of a legislative body. In absolute monarchy, there is little protection of people's natural or civil rights. In some cases, the monarch justifies his/her power by claiming it is based on divine right. France's **Louis XIV** is an example of a **divine right** ruler. Other rulers, such as Russia's **Catherine the Great** claimed to be **enlightened despots** (absolutists who use power for their people rather than for themselves).

- **Constitutional monarchy**, in which legal limits are placed on the power of the monarch. This can be done by a constitution, or, as is the case with Great Britain, by an "unwritten constitution" (a series of documents, laws, precedents, and legal equity). Sometimes constitutional monarchs are left with so little power that they become mere figureheads (Japan's emperor is an example).

Totalitarian Government

In **Totalitarian** governments, absolute decision making power is in the hands of a small group of leaders or a single dictator. Totalitarianism developed during the 20th Century. The technological developments of advanced transportation and communication systems enabled individuals and small groups to exercise enormous control.

In addition to nearly absolute political power, totalitarian governments control the economic, social, and cultural life of the people. Although constitutions may exist which seem to protect natural and civil rights, they are often shams. Imprisonment without a trial, censorship, limits on religious freedom, the elimination of political opposition, and summary executions are common. Totalitarian political philosophy is the opposite of democracy. In totalitarian systems, the citizen exists to serve the state.

Examples of totalitarian political structures include:

- **Fascist systems** are dictatorships built on near fanatical nationalism and military power. Hitler's Germany and Mussolini's Italy are examples of fascist totalitarian governments. Although both countries had constitutions and held plebiscites (elections), there was no real freedom or democratic expression. Private property continued in both countries, but government agencies made the basic economic decisions. The failure to protect natural and civil liberties is apparent in the anti-Semitism which culminated in the genocide of the Jews in Germany.

Hitler

Stalin

- **Communist totalitarian governments** such as those of the Soviet Union under Stalin or contemporary Red China also place decision making in the hands of an elite political group (party) from which one paramount leader often emerges. A constitution and elections also exist, but offer no protection of rights or freedom of democratic expression. The right to private property is abolished. All the means of production are owned by the government which makes economic decisions.

Brutal repression of opposition is common in totalitarian states. Ukrainian peasants who protested the Stalinist government's seizure of their land in the 1930's were tortured, killed, exiled to Siberia, or subjected to deliberate starvation.

World Issue ②

Revolution as a Modern Political Determinant

While political revolts against injustice are as old as humankind, **national revolutions** (forceful overthrow and replacement of an existing government by the people governed) are relatively modern. Revolution involves a complete change in a national political system, not just a replacement of a ruler.

Most significant revolutions go through several phases before achieving a new, long-lasting replacement system of government. Early phases are often in the hands of moderate reformers. Then, as the drive for change becomes widespread, more radical leaders emerge, and the intensity (and violence) increases. This emotionally-charged radical phase is often climactic and ushers in a more conservative phase in which a stronger, more stable form of government is finally established. The chart on the next page indicates some of the causes and results of some significant political revolutions.

National Revolutions in Modern Times

French Revolution (1789)

Causes:
Autocratic government (Louis XIV), near bankruptcy, disproportionate power of the clergy and nobility, unfair taxation, and Enlightenment philosophy (Voltaire, Rousseau) fed the discontent of the middle class (Third Estate/bourgeoise).

Results:
A more democratic form of government, merit-based government jobs, abolition of special privileges of clergy and nobility, rise of bourgeoise

Russian Revolution (1917)

Causes:
World War I, land hunger, autocratic Tsarist government, poor working conditions in factories

Results:
Withdrawal from WW I, peasant seizure of land, workers' seizure of factories, abolition of monarchy, government changed first to a republic, then to a Bolshevik oligarchy under Lenin

Chinese Revolution (1949)

Causes:
Need for land reform, corruption in the Nationalist government under Chiang Kai-shek, ongoing civil war, and chaos of World   War II

Results:
Initial redistribution of land, then collectivization, an end to the civil war, establishment of a communist government under Mao Zedong

Cuban Revolution (1959)

Causes:
Corruption of Batista government, need for land reform, anti-foreign sentiment

Results:
Land reform, nationalization of foreign wealth, establishment of a communist government under Castro

Iranian Revolution (1979)

Causes:
Struggle between modernization and traditionalism, need for land reform, poor distribution of wealth, resistance of Muslim fundamentalists under the Ayatollah Khomeini

Results:
Changes include: overthrow of autocratic monarchy, establishment of religious ruling group dominated by Khomeini (Islamic Republic), land reform, exile for the wealthy classes

World
Issue 3

Economic Systems

Economic systems are designed to make basic decisions about how scarce resources will be utilized and distributed. Economic systems usually reflect values and attitudes of the society's political decision makers. As with political systems, comparisons of the types of economic systems can be based on who makes the key decisions.

Characteristics of Basic Economic Systems

Traditional (ex.: India)

Decision Making:	*Problems:*
Custom, religion, and tradition determine many economic decisions.	Unable to deal with change; labor-intensive subsistence level of production; No surpluses to trade and obtain development capital.

Market — "Capitalist" or "free enterprise" (ex.: United States)

Decision Making:	*Problems:*
Individual decision making, consumer demand, and producer supply combine to make basic economic decisions. Private property and profit are vital. Minimal government involvement (laissez-faire) is desireable.	Inequality between income levels (classes); subject to unpredictable fluctuations of business activities. Early capitalists tended to exploit workers to cut costs and maximize profits. Some government regulation is usually needed for fairness,

Command (ex.: Communist China)

Decision Making:	*Problems:*
Central planning agency makes basic economic decisions of what to make, for whom, and for how much. Government controls most of the resources and means of production.	Lack of personal incentive to improve quality of life often leads to inadequate production and poor quality. Strong centralization limits flexibility of decision making.

Socialism (ex.: Great Britain)

Decision Making:	*Problems:*
Government planning agency makes some of the economic decisions, market and private businesses make others. Government owns some of the means of production. Extensive social welfare program.	High cost of extensive government social welfare programs results in high taxes which cut incentive.

Mixed Systems

Today, all economic systems are **mixed economies**. This means they blend elements of the different systems noted in the chart on page 80.

Some, such as the capitalist system of the United States, are predominantly market. However, the U.S. government ownership of the postal service and Amtrak and sponsorship of social welfare programs such as Social Security and Medicare are indications of socialism mixed into a capitalist system.

Others, such as the communist system of the China, are primarily command. The cooperative movement and provision for some private ownership of small businesses as well as the increasing use of incentives indicate that it is also a mixed economic system.

Additional Information on Political and Economic Systems

Consult your text on Political and Economic Systems. In *N&N's Global Studies Review Text,* more information on can be found in Section IV in each of the seven global units and on

India's traditional economy   [pgs. 83, 220]
China's command system   [pgs. 102, 104-106 109-112, 114-116, 120-123]
Britain's socialist system   [pgs. 43, 84, 218-219, 284-285]
Athenian dem)cr 1cy   [pg. 233]
Monarchy   [pgs. 247-250, 253, 262-263, 275-276, 308-309]
Parliamentary democracy   [pgs. 275-276, 138, 71]
Totalitarianism   [pgs. 112, 269-272, 320-322, 325-327]

Questions

Base your answer to question 1 on the cartoon at the right showing a group of Red Army soldiers and a dead student protestor and on your knowledge of social studies.

1   The cartoon above supports the idea that
   1   maintaining peace and order are the most important responsibilities of governments
   2   many young people cannot understand the value of democratic principles
   3   peaceful protests may not succeed in a totalitarian society
   4   totalitarian governments allow free expression of political ideas

2   The cartoon is referring to the problems that
   1   Deng Xiaoping faced in selecting his successor
   2   the communist world faced in dealing with political change
   3   Gorbachev faced with the Soviet economy
   4   Solidarity faced in its desire to align Poland with China

3   Which of the following economic systems is most commonly found in the world today?
   1   capitalism   3   mixed
   2   communism   4   traditional

4   Which political system provides the greatest protection for natural and civil rights?
   1   enlightened despotism   3   totalitarianism
   2   absolute monarchy   4   democracy

5   Which statement is correct?
   1   Democratic countries never change their political or economic systems.
   2   Democratic systems have the same characteristics.
   3   In a democratic system, the government exists to serve the people.
   4   Direct or pure democracy is the most common form of democracy today.

6   Absolute monarchy and totalitarianism are similar in that both
   1   place the interest of the individual citizen first
   2   fail to provide for hereditary succession to power
   3   fail to protect the natural and civil rights of the people
   4   have constitutions that effectively limit government power

7   Which belief is common to both 17th Century absolutism and
   20th Century totalitarianism?
   1   A two-party political system is essential for a stable society.
   2   Separation of church and state should be encouraged.
   3   Dissenters are dangerous and should be punished.
   4   The state should establish a strong public school system.

8   Which is the most valid statement about communism between WW II
   and Gorbachev's rule in the U.S.S.R.?
   1   national needs and goals shaped interpretations of communism
   2   all communist regimes strictly followed the same doctrine
   3   all communist nations loyally followed Soviet leadership
   4   communist expansion was limited to Eastern Europe

9   Which is characteristic of a traditional economic system?
   1   widespread use of machinery
   2   equal job opportunities for men and women
   3   intensive labor use
   4   heavy reliance on industrial income

10 The Magna Carta, the Glorious Revolution, and the Parliament
   Act of 1911 indicate that political change in Britain has occurred
   1   through a gradual evolutionary process
   2   as a result of pressure from the factory workers
   3   when the nobles defeated the king
   4   after the American Revolution

11 Which indicates a democratic method of choice?
   1   requirements that Spartan youth train as soldiers
   2   citizen discussion and voting on public matters in ancient Athens
   3   Soviet pressure on Eastern Europe to adopt communism after
      World War II
   4   establishment of Bantustans in South Africa

12 Which is a characteristic of totalitarian governments?
   1   Written constitutions and free elections are necessary for proper
      functioning of society.
   2   The rights of dissenters must be respected.
   3   Human rights should be guaranteed to all citizens.
   4   The requirements of the state are more important than the rights of
      individuals.

13 The political system of contemporary China is characterized by
   1   a strong central government
   2   rule by a coalition of emperors and religious leaders
   3   universal suffrage in national elections
   4   a strict adherence to constitutional principles

Model Essay

1   Certain political and economic systems are found together at various points in history.

Pairs

Absolutism - Mercantilism
Democracy - Capitalism
Totalitarianism - Communism

For each of the pairs above:

a   Explain *two* key characteristics of the political and economic systems.

b   Explain through the use of a specific example why *each* pair has been linked at one point in history. [5,5,5]

Pre-writing Strategy: Before you begin to write your answer in full sentences, lay out your preliminary information on the lines and grid below and on the next page.

Absolute Monarchy / Mercantilism	
System Characteristics:	*Example- How Systems are Linked:*
Hereditary ruler with nearly absolute power. The ruler can tax, make laws, appoint government officials, and declare war without the approval of a legislative body Natural and civil rights receive little protection. Mercantilism's goal is governmental increase of its wealth through policies such as colonial possessions, tariffs, quotas. Constant government interference in the economy makes absolutism an ideal political system to accompany it.	

Democracy / Capitalism	
System Characteristics: Democracy involves a high degree of individual participation in political decision making through the election process. Capitalism involves a high degree of personal decision making about the use of economic resources. Use of private property and freedom of enterprise allow individual decisions.	*Example- How Systems are Linked:*

Totalitarianism / Communism	
System Characteristics:	*Example- How Systems are Linked:* Communism involves government ownership of all productive resources and gives virtually all of the decision making power to a central agency. The Soviet Union under Stalin concentrated power in the hands of the ruler, allowed no private ownership of the means of production. GOSPLAN was established to make the economic decisions for the country. The concentration of power found in a totalitarian system makes a communist economic system possible.

After completing the grid, write out your answers in three separate paragraphs, using complete sentences.

Additional Practice Essays

It is suggested that you design and complete your own grid layouts as "pre-writing" exercises for these additional essays.

2   Various societies have chosen different economic systems to organize and coordinate the production and distribution of goods and services.

Economic Systems

Capitalism
Socialism
Communism
Traditional
Mixed

Select *three* of the economic systems. For *each* system selected:

· Describe the major characteristics of the system.

· Discuss a problem associated with the system. [5,5,5]

3   Major revolutions in history have been brought about by a variety of conditions. Several revolutions are listed below.

Revolutions

French Revolution, 1789
Russian Revolution, 1917
Chinese Revolution, 1949
Cuban Revolution, 1959
Iranian Revolution, 1979

a   Select *two* revolutions from the list. For *each* one chosen, discuss two conditions that helped to bring about that revolution. [5,5]

b   For *one* of the revolutions chosen in answer to *a*, discuss *two* conditions that resulted from that revolution. [5]

LESSON 9 Geography and Human Existence

Regions of the World

Geography influences human life. The climate, location, topography, and natural resources affect the development of a region. Geography influences the kinds of work people do and how they deal with other people. Geographic features shape the economy, politics and society of a region.

For example, river valleys provided a supportive environment in early times. Alluvial soils and plentiful supplies of water helped early farmers set up their societies. Rivers linked villages providing an infrastructure. Geography was a prime reason civilizations emerged along the banks of the Nile, the Yellow, the Indus, and the Tigris Rivers.

With favorable geographic conditions, civilization thrives. Temperate climates and good water supplies sustained Western Europe. Abundant mineral supplies provide a basis for industry and trade.

Geography can also present barriers to human development. In the history of Africa and Latin America, geographic features such as the Sahara Desert and Andes Cordillera isolated people and worked against national unity. The scattering of people on islands make unity difficult in the Pacific region.

Geographic isolation led to the growth of regional power in such places as Japan, the Balkans, and Southeast Asia.

Poor climate, scarcity of water, and mineral resources restrict development and threaten existence. Political life is unstable. Nations of the Sahara barely subsist and their governments are often in turmoil.

World Geographic Features and Their Influence on Human Existence

Geographic Feature	Influence	Regional Examples
Climate	Climate creates advantages or disadvantages in development of infrastructures and agriculture. It can invite or prevent invasion.	Long, harsh snowy winters of Russia provided some protection from invasion (Napoleon & Hitler failed)
Location	Nearness to trade routes and waterways allows economic opportunities and cultural diffusion. It can also expose region to invasion.	Island locations for Britain and Japan historically protected them from invasion and forged them into seafaring powers
Topography	The contours of the land help or hinder development and invite or prevent invasion.	Himalayas provided India protection from invasion. Monsoon driven rains hitting Himalayas created major river valleys where population centered.

The Northern European Plain provides excellent agricultural conditions from France to the Ukraine, but is a wide open invasion route for armies

Sahara and Kalahari made the interior of Africa hard to penetrate, and inhabitants adopted nomadic lives. |
| Water Resources | influence population distribution, transportation agricultural and economic development | Aquatic life from vast rivers such as the Amazon and Nile feed people, provide hydroelectricity, and irrigation for agriculture |
| Minerals And Timber | aid economic development, but also make region a target for invasions and imperialism. | Oil of the Persian Gulf makes ruling families wealthy, but the strategic need for petroleum also subjects them to global political pressures. |

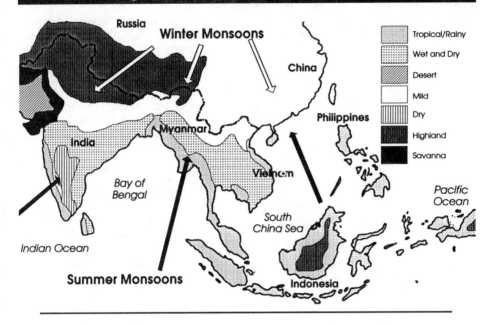

Climate:
Monsoon Winds of South Asia

Monsoon is an Arabic word meaning "seasonal wind." The lives of the people of India, Southern China, and the many neighboring nations of Southeast Asia depend on these winds.

The **summer monsoon winds** blow northward, off the Indian Ocean, bringing life-giving rains. South Asian farmers depend on them and adjust planting to their arrival. Late summer monsoons mean wasted seed and low crop yields. Early arrival means plowing and planting may not be completed. Heavy rains over long periods mean rotted crops and poor harvests. Floods often cause the Brahmaputra, Indus, Ganges, Irrawaddy, Mekong, and Huang Rivers to overflow and drive people from their homes.

Winter monsoon winds blow southward from the dry, cold interior of Asia. They can delay planting, shorten the growing season, and cut harvests. Winter monsoon winds are strong and dry. They cause much **erosion** (wearing away the topsoil).

Topography:
The Islands of Japan

Geographic factors play an important part in understanding the development of Japan. Japan is a North Pacific **archipelago** (island chain) extending 1500 miles north to south. Civilization developed on the three large islands in the south: Honshu, Shikoku, and Kyushu. The island topography isolated early Japan from invasion and commerce. Sporadic contact with China and Korea limited cultural diffusion.

Islands of Japan

A second topographic feature, Japan's *rugged mountainous terrain,* limits agriculture. The people rely on the sea for food supplies. The mountainous terrain made travel difficult and led to isolated communities dominated by **samurai** (local lords).

A third geographic factor, *lack of strategic mineral resources,* became important in modern times. The **Meiji Restoration** (1868) marked the beginning of industrialization. An alliance of military and business leaders took control of Japan. These leaders began a series of aggressive moves against neighboring nations to obtain needed coal, iron, oil and rubber. They launched wars against China (1894 and 1915) and Russia (1904) which gained them territorial rights and access to vital resources.

After World War I, this aggressive pattern accelerated. Japanese leaders followed the industrial patterns of Germany and Italy by increasing military production. Japan forced neighbors to join its **"Greater East Asia Co-Prosperity Sphere."** This was a trade alliance which fed Japan's industrial growth. To realize this scheme, Japan attacked China's mineral rich northern province of Manchuria (1931), China proper (1937), and Southeast Asia (1941). These actions created friction between Japan and the United States. The result was the attack on the United States Pacific Fleet at Pearl Harbor, Hawaii on 7 December 1941.

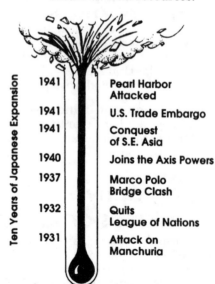

Ten Years of Japanese Expansion		
1941	Pearl Harbor Attacked
1941	U.S. Trade Embargo
1941	Conquest of S.E. Asia
1940	Joins the Axis Powers
1937	Marco Polo Bridge Clash
1932	Quits League of Nations
1931	Attack on Manchuria

Japanese Expansion Leads to Pearl Harbor

Water Resources:
Hydro–politics in the Middle East

For the people of the Middle East, the most critical element of existence is not petroleum, religion, or nationalism. It is a matter of water resources. The three major river basins in the region in the region are strained by the industry and agriculture needed to sustain the area's 200 million people. Demographic projections say that number will double in the next twenty-five years.

Even in the river basins, the scarcity of water is acute. International meetings to work out water sharing agreements began only recently. Turkey's Anatolian Plateau has significant water resources. Turkey's proposed pipeline projects of 1700 and 2400 miles in length are being examined. The projects require large amounts of financial and technological aid from industrial nations and the World Bank. Equally important is the cooperation of area nations that have had hostile relations for decades. Hydro–politics may be the one force that can bring a new age of peace to one of the most explosive regions on the globe.

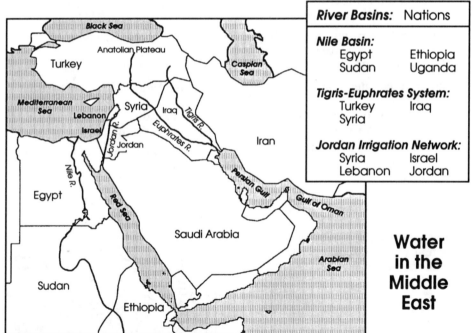

River Basins: Nations

Nile Basin:
Egypt	Ethiopia
Sudan	Uganda

Tigris-Euphrates System:
Turkey	Iraq
Syria	

Jordan Irrigation Network:
Syria	Israel
Lebanon	Jordan

Water in the Middle East

Additional Information
on Geography and Human Existence

Check your textbook on geographic influences. In *N&N's Global Studies Review Text*, review Section I of each regional unit for maps showing climate and topography; monsoons [pg. 57]; see also Unit 8 - World Today on environmental issues [pgs. 353-355]

Questions

1   Monsoons are seasonal winds that greatly influence life in
    1   North America   3   Latin America
    2   Eastern Europe   4   South Asia

2   River valleys created a supportive environment for early civilizations because they provided
    1   rich soil and plentiful supplies of water
    2   protection from invasion
    3   supplies of mineral resources
    4   shelter from monsoon winds

3   Rivers aided early cultural diffusion by providing
    1   hydro–politics   3   fish as a food source
    2   a variety of climates   4   an infrastructure

4   Great civilizations emerged along the banks of the Nile, the Yellow, the Indus, and the Tigris Rivers because of
    1   favorable geographic conditions
    2   cool climatic conditions
    3   abundant mineral supplies
    4   ease of defense against invasion

5   Western Europe was able to industrialize early because it had
    1   inadequate water supplies   3   mineral supplies available
    2   a temperate climate   4   a long rainy season

6   Japan forced neighbors to join its Greater East Asia Co-Prosperity Sphere to gain
    1   a pure water supply   3   access to industrial minerals
    2   protection from invasion   4   ease its overpopulation problems

7   For the people of the Middle East, the most critical element of existence is
    1   petroleum   3   nationalism
    2   religion   4   water resources

Base your answer to question 8 on the cartoon at the right and your knowledge of social studies.

8   The cartoon illustrates India's problems with
    1   inadequate transportation systems
    2   inefficient government agencies
    3   conflicts among religious groups
    4   monsoon cycles

Now, remove that and fix this one.

IBH Publishing Company Bombay.

9   Turkey's proposed pipeline projects require
    1   nuclear power   3   cooperation of area nations
    2   U.S. military protection   4   U.N. supervision

10   Mineral wealth can be valuable to a region, but it can also
    1   provide some protection from invasion
    2   force inhabitants to adopt nomadic lives
    3   make region a target imperialism
    4   promote cultural diffusion

Model Essay

1   Geographic factors can influence the development of a region of nation.

Geographic factors

Topography
Water resources
Climate
Natural resources
Location

Select three geographic factors from the list. For each factor selected, discuss how this factor had either a positive or negative effect on the development of Africa, Asia, Latin America, Europe, the Middle East, or a specific nation in one of those regions. You must use a different region for each factor selected. [5,5,5]

Pre-Writing Strategy: Before you begin to write your essay in full sentences, lay out your preliminary information on the grid format below.

Geographic Feature: Natural Resources	
Nation/Region: Japan	*Positive/Negative Effect:* Lack of iron, coal, oil and other minerals retarded early industrial growth. To obtain resources, leaders moved the country into aggressive actions against Korea, China, Russia, and Indochina

Geographic Feature: Location	
Nation/Region: India	*Positive/Negative Effect:* India is in the path of Monsoon Winds. The country's agriculture is highly dependent on rain bearing summer winds from the Indian Ocean. They have a positive effect if the timing is right. On the negative side, drought and famine occur if the wind pattern alters.

Geographic Feature: Water Resources	
Nation/Region: Middle East	*Positive/Negative Effect:* Water resources are more critical to existence than petroleum. The Nile, Tigris, and Jordan Basins are strained by the industry and agriculture needed to sustain this arid area's 200 million people.

Additional Practice Essay

2   Specific geographic features affect the history and policies of various nations.

Nations /features

Russia / lack of warm water ports
Japan / lack of mineral resources
Great Britain / large deposits of coal and iron ore
Iran / large deposits of petroleum
Panama / isthmus separating two oceans
Korea / location between China and Japan

Choose *three* of the nations listed above. For *each* one, explain how its geographic feature affected its history and policies. [5,5,5]

LESSON 10

Final Preparation For The Examination

Assignment 1

Read and compare the *Global Concepts* and the *World Issues* found on the charts on pages 96 through 99 with the concepts and issues reviewed in the previous 9 Lessons. It is also recommended that you use these charts as a guide for reviewing selected material from your text book.

Assignment 2

Study the *World Regions / "Have" and "Have Not" Nations* Map on page 100. a)Locate and label the World Regions (Africa, S.S.E. Asia, E. Asia, Latin America, Middle East, W. Europe, Russia and East Europe). b) In the boxes provided, describe the characteristics of the "Have" and "Have Not" nations.

Assignment 3

Review the **Glossary of Topically Related Terms** on pages 112 through 128. These terms should help you when preparing your "grids" for the essay questions. The terms are organized according to specific topics and include many more individuals, events, places, and concepts than are found in the 9 lessons.

Assignment 4

Read carefully the *Exam Strategy* on page 101. Apply the recommendations for taking the exam and use the "Grid" approach on Part II when completing the *Final Practice Exam* (pages 102-111). You should use the same guide lines when actually doing the *Examination in Global Studies*.

Concepts:	Examples:

Change
Variation or alteration of an existing situation...

- Effects of the Crusades
- French Revolution
- Independence for India
- Communes in China

Choice
Determining a preference for a particular idea or system, usually applies to economic decisions...

- former U.S.S.R.'s communist system
- Israel's mixed system
- China's economic development under Deng Xiaopong

Citizenship
The duties, rights, and privileges of a member of a state or nation...

- Direct democracy under Pericles in Athens
- Forces that have kept political participation from developing in Lat. Am.

Culture
The common concepts, habits, art, and institutions of a group of people...

- Influence of Confucian philosophy on Chinese civilization
- Russian Contributions to the Arts
- Golden Age of Muslim Culture

Diversity
Characterized by many different groups or situations...

- Variation of So. American landforms leads to a variety of life styles, crops, and separate cultures
- Geographic factors have promoted diversity in Western Europe

Empathy
To understand other people's problems and points of view ...

- Spanish missionary priests sought to understand and act to alleviate mistreatment of African slaves and Native American Indians

Environment
The conditions and circumstances surrounding a group or event...

- Rainfall shapes South Asian life
- Rapid urban growth in Latin America
- Vastness of Russia slowed its development

Concepts:	Examples:	
Human Rights Just and fair claims to natural, traditional, or legal powers and privileges...	• Treatment of races in South Africa • Jews in Nazi Germany • Treatment of students in Communist China	
Identity Feeling being able to share in the ideas and experiences of others...	• Islamic Fundamentalism • Myths and legends in African history	
Interdependence Being mutually influenced or controlled by similar forces...	• Economic development of Southeast Asia and Japanese trade • Marshall Plan aided post-WW II recovery in Europe	
Justice Fair and reasonable administration of laws; equitable behavior...	• Romans' Laws of the Twelve Tables • South Africa's racial problems	
Political Systems Specific structures for governing society...	• Evolution of British Parliamentary system • Power of the Communist Party in China • Communism in Latin America	
Power Capability to act decisively in situations...	• Japan's pre-World War II expansion • Rise of the Nazi State	
Scarcity Limits on quantities of goods and resources necessitating allocation and choices...	• Japan's dependence on other nations because of lack of critical petroleum resources • Middle East's economic development	
Technology Practical application of scientific principles for productive uses...	• India's future tied to technological development • Europe's industrialization	

World Issues

Issues:	Examples:

War and Peace

Economic and political conflicts and accommodations often have far-reaching consequences because of the intricate network of global relationships.

- Europe and the preludes to WW I
- Japan and the prelude to WW II
- Arab-Israeli Conflicts
- Cold War politics in Europe
- Discussion of changing political power structures in today's world

Population

Overpopulation not only has serious implications for the nation or region in which it occurs, but strains resources of others attempting to meet the increased economic demands. Conflicts arise as crowded nations seek more territory or as people migrate to more sparsely populated areas.

- India's population problems
- African Problems
- Discussion of world population pressures

Hunger and Poverty

The forces of industrialization, urbanization, and environmental depletion reveal inadequate food and resource distribution.

- Hunger in Africa
- Discussion of world hunger

Political and Economic Refugees

Resettlement of groups uprooted by wars, natural disasters, and industrialization causes stress and conflict throughout the globe.

- Africans and shanty-towns
- European refugees help Zionists establish Israeli State after WW II
- Palestinians

Economic Growth and Development

Technological progress brings increased contact among people. It forces re-evaluation of traditional life-styles. A mixture of systems for making economic decisions has resulted from international contacts.

- India's economic development
- A mixed economy in Israel
- Discussion of economic development in today's world
- Latin American development
- The British economy

Environmental Concerns

Devastation of the land and sea by natural and human forces has repercussions beyond a particular region because the scarcity of critical resources intensifies competition for them elsewhere.

- Desertification of Sahel in Africa
- European Efforts
- Discussion of environmental issues

Human Rights

Freedoms enjoyed by some societies are not shared by all. As international contact broadens, common expectations for human decency and justice rise.

- Apartheid in South Africa
- Hungarian Revolution
- Discussion of human rights in today's world

World Trade and Finance

Interaction of economic needs and desires demonstrate the interdependence among nations.

- Divestiture over Apartheid
- Discussion of economic development and world trade

Determination of Political and Economic Systems

Transfer of decision-making power among groups alters internal and external structure.

- Chinese Cultural Revolution
- French Revolution
- Central planning - former U.S.S.R.
- Discussion of changing political power structures in today's world

Energy: Resources and Allocations

The competition of industrially developed and developing nations for limited supplies of fossil fuels create global political and economic strains. The danger and limitations of artificially produced fuels create worldwide stresses.

- OPEC
- Discussion of energy resources in today's world

Geography – Human Existence

Geography influences human life. It influences jobs, customs, and human relationships. Geography shapes economy, politics, and society. Climate, location, topography, and natural resources affect development.

- Monsoons of South Asia
- Topography of Japan
- Conflicts over natural resources
- Hydro-politics of the Middle East

Regions of the World
"Have" and "Have Not" Nations

North Pacific Ocean

South Pacific Ocean

Australia

Indian Ocean

Arctic Ocean

North Atlantic Ocean

South Atlantic Ocean

"Have Not" Nations

"Have" Nations

"Have" Nations

"Have Not" Nations

Examination Strategies

How you approach the final exam and how you use your time can often affect your success.

· **Take the full amount of time:** You've spent a great deal of time and effort getting ready for the exam. A few minutes taken at the end can help you spot errors and make appropriate adjustment.

· **First Reading:** Skim over the whole examination quickly. Answer only those Part I questions of which you are absolutely sure. Skip the rest. When you get to Part II, read the questions and jot down on scrap paper any pieces of factual data you think you might use to answer the question. Do this for *each* question on Part II. It will help you decide which questions to choose to write.

· **Second Reading:** Read Part I again, but more slowly this time. Answer as many questions as you can, but don't be afraid to leave an answer blank for now. As you go through Part I this time, be alert for ideas which you might use in your Part II answers. Jot them down on scrap paper as they come to mind.

· **Write a Part II Answer:** Choose the Part II question about which you feel most confident and write the answer. Be brief. Let the point values guide you on how much to write. Written answers should not be more than two pages. Be sure to label the parts of the answer exactly as they are on the examination.

· **The Regents Exam lists these instructions for Part II:**

1) include specific factual information wherever possible.
2) keep to the questions asked; do not go off on a tangent.
3) avoid over-generalizations and sweeping statements which are difficult to prove.
4) keep these general definitions in mind:
   a. <u>discuss</u> means "to make observations about something using facts, reasoning, and arguments; to present in some detail"
   b. <u>describe</u> means "to illustrate something in words or tell about it"
   c. <u>show</u> means "to point out; to set forth clearly a position or idea by stating it and giving data which support it"
   d. <u>explain</u> means "to make plain or understandable; to give reasons for or causes of; to show the logical development or relationships of"

· **Third Reading:** Go back to Part I and work briefly on the remaining questions, then write out the remaining two Part II answers using the same guidelines as above.

· **Fourth Reading:** Finish Part I. Take your best guess on any questions of which you are unsure. *Do not leave any answer spaces blank.* Re-read all your answers on Part II carefully, and make corrections and alterations neatly. *Make sure all parts of each answer are properly and distinctly labeled.*

Practice Exam in Global Studies
Part I
ANSWER ALL QUESTIONS ON THIS PART
*(Many questions have been identified with their **Global Concept** in order to illustrate how the Key Concepts may be used to help answer the question.)

1   *[political systems] Which was common to both European and Japanese feudalism?
   1   widespread flourishing of commerce
   2   rapid development of industry and technology
   3   cultural diversity
   4   decentralized government

Base your answers to questions 2 through 4 on the case study below of a hypothetical society at three stages in its development and on your knowledge of social studies.

Stage A: People live in communal village settings. Because villages are self-sufficient, there is little need to travel far from the village, nor for others to come into the village. There is a strong physical resemblance among the people. Life styles show a high degree of similarity.

Stage B: New interest develops in this society about ideas and things of the wider world. Over a period of time, the economy shifts from subsistence to commercial. The familiar setting and ways of the village are being replaced by urban conditions and the ways of doing things are being transformed. Movement among communities is taking place.

Stage C: Economy is now based on industry and commerce. Economic, political, and social attitudes reflect the mobility of the population. Urban conditions prevail everywhere. Differences in physical appearances and lifestyles are evident.

2   [change] During which stages will the importation of textiles, food, and building materials most probably take place?
   1   *A* and *B*, only   3   *A* and *C*, only
   2   *B* and *C*, only   4   *A*, *B*, and *C*

3   [change] During which stage or stages of development will the people most likely be living in harmony with a single religious system?
   1   *A* only   3   *C* only
   2   *B* only   4   *A*, *B*, and *C*

4   [change] During which stage or stages of development will living in extended families be most commonplace?
   1   *A* only   3   *C* only
   2   *B* only   4   *A*, *B*, and *C*

5   **[identity]** *"A person should gladly go to jail when he breaks a law which he truly believes is unjust."* Which historic figure would identify with this statement?
   1   Sulieman the Magnificent   3   Mohandus Gandhi
   2   Peter the Great   4   Mao Zedong

Base your answer to question 6 on the cartoon at the right and on your knowledge of social studies.

6   The cartoonist is indicating that the new frontiers of tomorrow will be governed by advances in

   1   military production.
   2   developing nations.
   3   technology.
   4   human rights.

7   **[choice]** Which indicates a democratic method of choice?
   1   discrimination against non-whites in the Republic of South Africa
   2   soviet pressures on Eastern Europe to adopt communism after World War II
   3   citizen discussion and voting on public matters in ancient Athens
   4   requirements that Spartan youth train as soldiers

8   **[citizenship]** Which citizenship quality is most critical in democratic societies?
   1   high literacy rate
   2   unquestioning obedience
   3   support for the military
   4   the virtue of thrift

9   **[culture]** In Chinese history prior to the 20th century, cultural traditions were transmitted primarily by the
   1   government
   2   family
   3   schools
   4   influence of foreigners

10   **[diversity]** The fact that the British parliamentary system has been diffused to many nations throughout the world is best explained by the
   1   political and economic power of present-day Britain
   2   adaptability of British culture to all situations.
   3   universal respect shown to royalty and judicial institutions.
   4   adoption of British institutions by its former colonies.

11 [choice] To organize scarce resources, all societies must develop economic systems to
1   make choices on how to use their resources.
2   maintain traditional religious practices.
3   pass on the basic cultural values to their young.
4   control the movement of people within the society.

12 [political systems] Which is characteristic of totalitarian societies?
1   religious worship is forbidden.
2   citizens are denied the right to vote.
3   governments control mass media.
4   governments yield to the demands of the citizens.

13 [empathy] The Russian peasants supported the 1917 Bolshevik revolution mainly because the Bolsheviks seemed to empathize with the peasants desire for
1   control of their land.
2   defeat of the German invaders.
3   freedom of religion.
4   new factory jobs for all citizens.

Base your answer to question 14 on the chart at the right and on your knowledge of social studies.

Country	Population (millions)	Percent Literate	Years of Life Expectancy
Japan	118	99%	74.7
India	690	36%	41.1
China	1048	70%	62.5
Italy	52	94%	71.9
Spain	38	93%	72.3

14 [technology] Which of the following conclusions does the chart support?
1   High literacy rates are found only in Europe.
2   Large populations always have low literacy rates.
3   High literacy rates appear to be related to life expectancy.
4   Italy appears to have the highest standard of living.

15 [identity] Which would reflect a rejection of colonialism and an attempt to establish cultural identity?
1   Egypt and Israel signing a peace treaty.
2   Nigeria joining the United Nations.
3   Nicaragua's accepting military aid from the former U.S.S.R.
4   Nationalist leaders changing the Republic of the Congo's name to Zaire.

16   **[environment]** Which factor has the greatest influence on food production in India?
1   high demand by other nations for grain
·2   irrigation projects in the Deccan plateau
3   natural effects of the monsoon winds
4   government support for technological development

17   **[political systems]** Which is the most valid statement about communism during the years between World War II and Gorbachev's rule in the former U.S.S.R.?
1   Most communist nations rejected Soviet leadership in world affairs
2   The Soviet Union dictated the foreign policies of the Third World
3   Differing national needs and goals altered strict Marxist doctrine
4   Communism ended in the world when the Soviet Union dissolved

18   **[interdependence]** The European Economic Community and the Latin American Trade Association
1   prohibit trade with non members
2   control world prices for certain products
3   compete with the United Nations
4   promote economic development in their regions

19   **[human rights]** Historically, human rights received little emphasis in Asian societies because in Asia
1   most societies were not literate.
2   centralized governments were rare.
3   the welfare of the society superseded individual rights.
4   internal conflicts prevented political stability.

20   **[power]** Which is a major reason that the United Nations has often been unsuccessful in solving international disputes?
1   The United Nations does not have sufficient funds to act.
2   The disputing members are usually not members of the United Nations.
3   National sovereignty prevents international cooperation.
4   The United Nations Charter does not provide a means to settle disputes.

21   **[change]** The Russian Revolution of November 1917 and the French Revolution of 1789 are similar in that both
1   returned a monarch to power.
2   experienced periods of violence and internal disorder.
3   led to government ownership of all economic resources.
4   promoted the idea of democracy.

22   **[technology]** Rapid technological progress usually results in
1   economic isolation
2   social & economic change
3   preservation of tradition
4   broadening of human rights

Base your answers to questions 23 through 26 on the chart (right) and on your knowledge of social studies.

Percent of Top U.S. Corporations With Foreign Operations		
Total in	Current	Planned for 1990's
Europe	67%	+16%
Canada, South & Central America	64%	+42%
Asia	18%	+56%
Australia & New Zealand	8%	+ 2%
Africa	2%	-
Middle East	1%	+ 3%
India	-	+ 3%
Other	1%	+ 2%

23 [interdependence] Which conclusion is most valid from looking at where current corporations are located?
1 The developed nations are primarily in the Northern Hemisphere.
2 There is an even distribution of manufacturing facilities throughout the world.
3 The U.S. has its strongest economic ties in the Middle East and Africa.
4 Colonial possessions are important to American business.

24 [interdependence] Which of the following will probably happen in the 1990's if the projections in the "planned" column become reality
1 many new nations will achieve independence.
2 the conflict between communism and democracy will intensify.
3 world hunger will be substantially reduced.
4 cultural diffusion will be increased.

25 [interdependence] One reason for the substantial increase in United States corporations' interest in Asian development is
1 a strong similarity of cultural traditions in America and Asia.
2 improved diplomatic relations with People's Republic of China.
3 dominance of capitalism and democracy throughout East Asia.
4 the long history of isolationism in Japan and China.

26 Which of the concepts is best reflected in the chart as a whole?
1 isolationism   3 interdependence
2 self-reliance   4 political systems

27 [scarcity] Which is the most accurate conclusion about the food shortage in Africa in the last half of the 20th century?
1 African farmers are inefficient.
2 Colonial rulers weakened most African economies.
3 Natural disasters and human mismanagement are to blame.
4 Too few Africans work in the agricultural sector.

28 [justice] In Latin America, the administration of justice has often been compromised by
1 rough, mountainous topography.
2 movement of rural people into urban centers.
3 diffusion of power among numerous caudillos.
4 intense racial segregation.

Base your answers to questions 29 through 31 on the speakers' statements below and on your knowledge of social studies.

Speaker A:
A government should own all the resources of production and allocate them as it determines what is in the best interests of the state.

Speaker B:
A government should not interfere in the economy, and it should allow the market to determine what to produce and how much to produce.

Speaker C:
A government should own some means of production, but allow some private ownership. It should also promote a national program of social welfare.

Speaker D:
A government should allow private ownership, but exercise a high degree of control in order to promote the interests of the state.

29 **[political systems]** Speaker *B* reflects the ideas associated with
1 Islamic fundamentalism.
2 laissez-faire capitalism.
3 socialism.
4 divine right rule.

30 **[political systems]** Speaker *A* best expresses ideas similar to the
1 mercantilists of Europe in the 17th and 18th centuries.
2 leaders of the anti-apartheid movement.
3 ideas associated with the Bolshevik leaders of the Russian Revolution.
4 members of the Palestinian Liberation Organization.

31 **[political systems]** The economic direction being taken by the leadership of the Peoples' Republic of China in the past decade is from an economic system based on
1 *A's* ideas to one resembling those of *C*.
2 *B's* ideas to one resembling those of *A*.
3 *D's* ideas to one resembling those of *A*.
4 *B's* ideas to one resembling those of *C*.

32 **[change]** As a force for change in modern African societies, urbanization has led to a decline in the importance of
1 literacy.   3 extended families.
2 medical care.   4 technology.

33 **[diversity]** Which statement about the Islamic world reflects the concept of cultural diversity?
1 Religious unity has created strong political unity.
2 The only Islamic nations in the world are in the Middle East.
3 All Islamic nations are committed to the destruction of Israel.
4 Significant religious and political differences exist among Islamic sects.

34   **[empathy]** Empathy for European Jews who suffered the horror of the Nazis' genocidal "final solution" (holocaust) has led many nations to
1   track down former Nazi death camp officials.
2   close their borders to Jewish immigrants.
3   oppose the existence of a Jewish homeland in the Middle East.
4   support efforts to build up Israeli military power.

35   **[power]** Which was a characteristic of Western European nations that most enabled them to establish colonies in Asia and Africa?
1   rigid social class structures
2   self-sufficiency in natural resources
3   frequent political revolutions
4   advanced technology

36   **[interdependence]** In the past 50 years, which of the following indicates a growing trend toward global interdependence?
1   banks in developed nations making loans to Third World countries
2   attempts by France to retain its colonies in Southeast Asia
3   Islamic fundamentalists in Iran protesting against Western influence
4   movement of rural Latin Americans to urban areas

37   **[scarcity]** Scarcity of natural resources in the major industrial nations of Europe in the 19th century and in Japan in the 20th century moved them toward
1   imperialistic conquest.
2   feudal systems.
3   agricultural revolutions.
4   importation of slave labor.

38   **[human rights]** Which is the clearest violation of the international values expressed in the 1948 United Nations' *Declaration of Human Rights* and the Helsinki Accords of 1975?
1   the overthrow of Ferdinand Marcos' regime in the Philippines
2   the apartheid policies of the Republic of South Africa
3   the glasnost policy of Mikhail Gorbachev in the former U.S.S.R.
4   the goals of Sun Yat-sen in establishing the Republic of China

39   **[culture]** The best evidence that Africa has been greatly influenced by the diffusion of Western values is that many African nations are
1   strengthening the traditional extended family.
2   making efforts to increase the power of landlords.
3   increasing the power of tribal chiefs.
4   using parliamentary governmental structures.

40   **[political systems]** A valid generalization about democracy is that, although it exists in many different forms, it is always characterized by a
1   presidential form of government.
2   toleration of political opposition.
3   two-party system.
4   powerful executive.

Base your answer to question 41 on the graph at the right and on your knowledge of social studies.

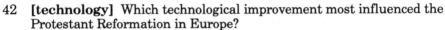

Real & Projected Population Growth

41 **[change]** According to the graph, the world's population
1 will have its fastest growth in Asia.
2 saw the greatest increase in the 1960's.
3 will exceed the food supply in the 1990's.
4 will be more than double that of 1960 by the year 2000.

42 **[technology]** Which technological improvement most influenced the Protestant Reformation in Europe?
1 compass
2 gunpowder
3 telescope
4 printing press

43 **[environment]** In which of the following ways has the physical environment played a role in the history of the former Soviet Union?
1 long, harsh winters have hindered invasions by outsiders
2 lack of resources has limited development
3 high mountains have hindered cultural diffusion
4 accessible natural harbors have increased trade

44 **[change]** Mohandus K. Gandhi, Jomo Kenyatta, and Simon Bolivar
1 helped their homelands achieve independence.
2 used non-violent passive resistance to injustice.
3 promoted westernization and industrialization.
4 advocated cultural diversity and diffusion.

45 Historically, the general isolation of Japan helped to develop a common language, history, government, customs, and traditions. These factors contributed to Japan's
1 unique cultural identity.
2 religious diversity.
3 present position as a major global trading power.
4 reliance on Middle East petroleum.

46 *"We live in a time when the knowledge of world affairs is no longer simply nice to have or a luxury. It is essential to a nation's well-being."* This statement is based on a recognition of the crucial role in today's world of
1 religious fundamentalism.
2 interdependence.
3 imperialism.
4 isolationism.

47 *"The Andes have isolated the Inca culture and defeated Bolivar's dream of a united South America."* This statement indicates
1 fighting over rich natural resources undermines nationalism.
2 the importance of language and religion in the modern nation-state.
3 cultural diversity is aided by productive agriculture.
4 the natural environment shapes human development.

PART II
ANSWER THREE QUESTIONS FROM THIS PART

1   [change] While social, political, and economic change is a familiar
     reality in most countries throughout the world, it does not always come
     easily or without resistance. Societal change can be rapid or slow,
     widespread or limited, long lasting or temporary.

Countries

· India   · Nicaragua   · Japan
· Poland   · Iran   · Republic of South Africa

Identify or describe a societal change that has occurred since World War
II in *three* of the countries listed above. For *each* country chosen,
discuss *one* force that has acted to promote the change described, *and*
one force that has acted as a barrier to that change. You must use a
different change for each country chosen. [5,5,5]

2   [justice] Justice in the 20th century includes the idea that all people
     have human rights which, like natural rights and civil rights, should be
     protected by governments. Select *three* of the following national leaders.
     For *each* leader chosen, discuss the degree of justice that existed under
     his administration. [5,5,5]

National Leaders

· Germany - Hitler   · Republic of So. Africa - Botha
· Soviet Union - Stalin   · Mexico - Juarez
· Iran - Khomeini   · Kampuchea - Pol Pot
· Byzantine Empire - Justinian

3   [environment] The geographic environment greatly influences the
     lives of people throughout our world.

People

· rice farmers in Southeast Asia
· cattle herders in Argentina
· oil refinery workers in Saudi Arabia
· terrace farmers in China
· coffee growers in Columbia
· nomads of North Africa
· cotton farmers in India's Deccan Plateau
· wheat farmers in Ukraine

Choose *three* of the groups of people listed above. For *each* one chosen:

·   Identify a specific geographic factor which affects the lives of these
      people, and explain how it affects them.
·   Explain whether the geographic factor is a positive *or* negative force
      in their lives. [5,5,5]

4   **[human rights]**   Below is a list of violations of human rights that have occurred throughout history.

Violations of Human Rights

- Repression of dissidents
- Genocide
- Destruction of cultural heritage
- Denial of civil and legal rights
- Forced relocation

a   Select *three* of the types of violations from the list above. For *each* one chosen, describe a historical example of that violation, including the approximate time period and place. You must use a *different* example for each violation discussed. [4,4,4]

b   Show how a specific group or organization, public or private, has promoted the cause of human rights. [3]

5   **[interdependence]**   Many problems today can be considered global problems because their existence in one country or region affects others in the world. Some of these *problems* are:

- Scarcity of energy resources
- Spread of nuclear armaments
- Lack of investment capital
- Terrorism
- Poverty

Choose *three* of the problems listed above. For *each* one chosen:

- Show how that problem is a global problem, since its existence in one specific country or region affects others in the world.
- Discuss how attempts to deal with the problem have caused nations to cooperate. [5,5,5]

6   **[identity]**   A sense of identity is crucial to human existence and understanding.

Identities

- a serf on a medieval European manor
- a peasant on a present-day Chinese commune
- an apprentice under the guild system in 15th century Europe
- a present-day factory worker in Japan
- a black diamond mine worker in the Republic of South Africa
- a campesino on a Mexican encomienda around 1900
- a factory worker in England in the early 19th century

Assume the identity of *three* of the individuals listed above. For *each* one chosen, have the person describe their life situation and discuss one advantage and one disadvantage of the life they lead. [5,5,5]

Glossary of Topically Related Terms

Note: *This comprehensive list of factual data and definitions goes beyond the limited examples presented in the nine lessons of this book. The items correspond with the most common themes for exam questions. Use this glossary to add data to your practice essays.*

War, Terrorism, and Peace Political and Economic Refugees

Appeasement – policy of giving in to aggressors to avoid war

Arafat, Yassir – leader of Palestine Liberation Organization

Armada –Philip II Spanish invasion fleet defeated by England, 1588

Atlantic Charter –(1941) Allies' WW II aims; basis for U.N. Charter

Austro-Prussia War – (1866) Bismarck used war to unify Germany

Balance of Power – diplomatic alliances to kept peace in 19th C. Europe

Balfour Declaration – WW I British promise of Israeli nationhood

Battle of Britain – Hitler's relentless air attacks on British, 1940-41

Battle of Midway – 1942 sea battle considered to be turning point for U.S. in Pacific theater of WW II

Battle of Tours –Ended Muslim invasion of W. Europe, 8th C. A.D.

Battle of Vienna – (1683) Ottoman expansion into E. Europe ended

Battle of Waterloo –(1815) final defeat of Napoleon

Berlin Airlift – (1948) successful Cold War attempt by Allies to supply German city cut off by Soviets

Berlin Conference –(1884-85) African territorial claims partially worked out by Europeans

Berlin Wall – built by Soviets in 1960's to deter escapes from communist zone of the city; dismantling began in 1989, as democratic reforms began to sweep Eastern Europe

Bloody Sunday – period of violence during the Russian Revolution, 1905

Blitzkrieg –Nazis' "lightning war" surprise attack tactics used in WW II

Boxers –anti-imperialist group led rebellion in China, 1900

Camp David Accords – 1979 peace agreements by Egypt and Israel

Carter, Jimmy – U.S. President 1977-1981; engineered 1970's Camp David Mid-East peace agreements

Central Intelligence Agency (CIA) – U.S. espionage & counter terrorist operations

Cheka –Tsarist Russian secret police involved in Balkan terrorism

Christian Phalangists –political faction in Lebanese civil war

Churchill, Winston –British Prime Minister during WW II

Cold War –clash between U.S. and U.S.S.R. in post-WW II Europe

Concert of Europe – 19th C. int'l organization est. to preserve peace

Congress of Vienna – (1815) organized the restoration of political power in Europe after the defeat of Napoleon,

Conquistadores – Spanish conquerors of Lat. Am. Indian lands, set up colonial rule

Contadora Group –(1980's) leaders of Central American republics seeking solutions to the violence in Central America

Continental System –Napoleonic trade regulations of 1806 to hurt British trade and to help France establish economic supremacy

Contras – (1980's) rebel group against communist rule in Nicaragua

Coup d'état – military overthrow of the governments

Crimean War –(1854) cost Russia much Balkan territory

Crusades – (1095-1291) attempts by various Medieval Christian nobles to win back Jerusalem and its surrounding regions from Muslims

Détente – cordial diplomatic atmosphere between former adversaries

Diaspora – dispersion of the Jews from Palestine, c. 70 A.D.

Dienbienphu – (1954) final defeat of French colonialism in Vietnam

Domino Theory –theory that communist victory in one state would lead to other nations falling

Easter Rebellion – (1916) Irish uprising v. British, led to independence

Fourteen Points - WW I peace plan drawn up by President Wilson, 1918

Franco-Prussian War – (1871) victory enhanced prestige of new German state under Bismarck

Gaza Strip –Mediterranean coastal territory taken from Egypt by Israel in the 1967 war; troubled site of Palestinian refugee settlements

Geneva Agreements – (1954) provided for an independent and neutral Indochinese states after French defeat

Genocide – deliberate elimination of a racial or cultural group

Golan Heights – strategic border territory taken from Syria in 1967 Arab-Israeli War

Gorbachev, Mikhail – Soviet reform leader; negotiated end to Cold War; ended Soviet dominance of Eastern Europe; began *glasnost* democratic constitutional reforms and *peristroika* economic reforms; resigned Soviet Presidency with the collapse of the U.S.S.R. in 1991

Great Wall of China –built as an invasion defense on northern borders of China in Quin period, c. 220 B.C.

Hague Conferences – pre-WW I, attempt.to limit arms race

Hiroshima – Japanese industrial city, atom bomb target, 1945

Hitler, Adolf – fascist dictator of Nazi Germany, 1933-45

Holocaust –Nazi genocide against Jews, 1933-1945

Imperialism – political and economic control of a nation over other groups or territories

Indo-Pakistani Wars –border disputes over Punjab, Kashmir, since 1948

Iran-Iraq War – (1980-1989) bloody confrontation over Muslim fundamentalism and border territories

Irish Republican Army (IRA) –militant group seeking independence for Northern Ireland; "Provisional Wing" of IRA engaged in terrorism

Iron Curtain – Churchill coined the phrase to describe the prevention the free flow of ideas between the West and the communist dominated Eastern Europe

Jerusalem – center of Muslim-Christian conflicts (Crusades to present)

Jihad – Islamic holy war

Johnson, Lyndon – U.S. President, escalated Vietnam War, 1965-68

Kaiser Wilhelm II –German monarch, c. WW I

Kennedy, John F. – U.S. President 1961-1963; Cuban Missile Crisis v. Khrushchev of U.S.S.R.; founded Peace Corps

Kellogg-Briand Pact – 1928 Pact of Paris proposed a worldwide non-aggression structure

Knights – land-holding nobles became warrior class under Europe's medieval feudal system

Korean War – (1950-53) Major military conflict of Cold War; U.S. and U.N. attempted to contain aggressive actions of N. Koreans backed by Red China and U.S.S.R.

Kuomintang – Nationalist Party in 20th C. Chinese Civil War

League of Nations –world peace organization after WW I; weakly condemned German, Italian, and Japanese aggression in 1930's

Limited Nuclear Test Ban Treaty – (1963) no atomic tests in atmos.

MacArthur, Douglas –American military commander, WW II & Korea; supervised post-war occupation of Japan

Manchuria –territorial conflict: Japan v. Russia. c. 1905

Mare Nostrum – Mussolini's expansionist program to restore Fascist Italy as a power in Mediterranean, c. 1930's

Marshall Plan –European Recovery Act, 1947-1951; sent $12 billion in U.S. aid to rebuild Western Europe

Mau Mau - Kenyan terrorist group in 1950's

Monroe Doctrine –(1823) U.S. policy warned European nations against re-establishing colonies in Latin America; basis for subsequent U.S. intervention in Latin America

Munich Conference –(1938) summit meeting at which Britain and France appeased Hitler, yielding Czech territory

Mussolini, Benito – Italian fascist dictator, 1922-40's

Nagasaki –site of 2nd atomic bomb dropped by U.S. in 1945

Napoleon I (Bonaparte) –Emperor of France in early 1800's; extensive conquests in Europe

Napoleonic Code –legal system of 19th C. French Empire; became basis for modern laws in much of Europe

Nationalism –a strong feeling of unity for people who desire to control their own destinies

Nationalization – government takeover of private business from owners

Nazi-Soviet Non-Aggression Pact – (1939) Stalin, Hitler agreed not to attack each other, and secretly planned to divide Poland

Nixon, Richard – U.S. President 1969-74; intensified U.S. involvement in Vietnam, then set up withdrawal

Non-alignment –neutralist position in which a nation refuses to always be allied on same side in all issues

North Atlantic Treaty Organization (NATO) – Western European, Canadian, and U.S. defense agreement, (1949 – present)

Nuclear Nonproliferation Treaty – (1968) attempted to stop spread of nuclear weapons to countries not already having them

Nuclear Test Ban Treaty – (1963) U.S., U.S.S.R., and eventually 62 other nations agreed to cease nuclear tests in atmosphere

Orders in Council –British response to trade restrictions of Napoleonic Continental System

Organization of American States (OAS) –mutual assistance league for U.S. & Latin American nations (1947 – present)

Outer Space Treaty –(1967) prohibited nuclear weapons in outer space

Palestinian Liberation Organization (PLO) – seeks separate Palestinian Arab state in areas occupied by Israel; involved in terrorist activities; headed by Yassir Arafat

7/27

- **Pax Romana** – domination of ancient Mediterranean world by the Romans, c. 35 B.C. - 135A.D.
- **Peace Corps** – American volunteer program for educational, agricultural, and industrial development in Third World nations, launched in 1961 by U.S. President Kennedy

Peaceful Coexistence – Khrushchev's 1960's foreign policy of minimizing confrontations with Western powers; continued by Brezhnev; laid basis for Détente of 1970's

- **Pearl Harbor** – U.S. naval base in Hawaii attacked by Japan in 1941

Potsdam Conference – (1945) disagreements among WW II Allies left Europe divided into two hostile segments - communist v. democratic

- **Qaddafi, Muammar** –Libyan military leader overthrew the monarchy in 1969; used vast oil reserves to promote terrorism and revolutionary politics in Middle East

Red Brigades – (Italy) communist terrorist activities 1969-present

Red Guards –Mao mobilized Chinese students as terrorist purge factions in 1960's Cultural Revolution

- **Reign of Terror** –most violent period of French Revolution in mid-1790's when 15-45,000 alleged opponents of the Revolution were executed

Rome-Berlin-Tokyo Axis – (1939) alliance of three of the aggressor nations of the world

- **Roosevelt, Franklin D.** –U.S. President, 1933-45; WW II leader: Atlantic Charter; Yalta Conf.; U.N. Charter; shaped post WW II era
- **Roosevelt, Eleanor** –chaired commission for U.N. on human rights 1947-1960; produced universal *Declaration of Human Rights*
- **Roosevelt, Theodore** – U.S. President, 1901-09; Panama Canal, Big Stick Policy in Latin America
- **Russo-Japanese War** – world power structure altered in 1904-1905 when Japan emerged as major nation

Sadat, Anwar – Egyptian President signed Camp David Accords with Israel; assassinated 1981

- **SALT (Strategic Arms Limitation Treaties)** – U.S., U.S.S.R.; SALT I placed limits on certain types of missiles; SALTII placed limits on delivery vehicles, warheads, but U.S. Senate did not ratify because of its concerns over Soviet activities in Cuba and Afghanistan

- **Samurai** –feudal warrior class in Japan

Savak – Iranian Shah's hated secret police

Scorched-Earth Policy –retreat-and-destroy tactics used by Russians to defeat Napoleonic and Nazi invaders

- **S.E.A.T.O.** – Southeast Asia Treaty Organization; U.S. sponsored multi-lateral defense agreement, 1954-1974

Sepoy Rebellion – (1858) Hindu and Moslem mutiny against British

- **Shi'ites** – Muslim fundamentalist sect; led Iranian Revolution, 1979; associated with terrorist actions in Middle East

- **Shogun** –most powerful military overlord of Japanese feudal era
- **Sinai Peninsula** –Middle East; conquered by Israel in 1967 war; returned to Egypt by Camp David agreement
- **Sino-Japanese War** – (1894-95) ended Chinese power claims in E. Asia

Space Race –space exploration became 1960's Cold War struggle

"SS" – Germany's Nazi secret police violated human rights, discouraged opposition

Strategic Defense Initiative (SDI) – referred to as "Star Wars;" proposed U.S. space-based missile defense system; a stumbling block to U.S.-Soviet arms reduction negotiations during Reagan years (1980's)

Suez Canal –crisis occurred when nationalized by Nasser in 1956; put pressure on Western European nations

Teheran Conference –(1943) WW II Allied summit meeting of Stalin, FDR, and Churchill

Tel Aviv Airport – site of 1973 attack in Israel by Japanese terrorists working with the PLO

Terrorism –systematic use of violence to force a group to gain power

Treaty of Brest-Litovsk –(1917) Bolsheviks signed peace with the Germans; removed Russia from WW I

Treaty of Kanagawa –(1854) Japan-U.S. agreement, opened trade

Treaty of Tordesillias –(1494) set up by Pope in to divide colonial regions of Spain and Portugal

Treaty of Versailles –(1919) ended WW I; noted for harsh treatment of Germany and establishment of League of Nations

Triple Alliance –pre-WW I: Germany, Austria-Hungary, Italy

Triple Entente –pre-WW I alliance of France, Russia, Britain

Truman, Harry S. – U.S. Pres.; Marshall Plan and aid programs for under-developed nations to contain communist insurgency after WW II

Truman Doctrine –(1947) designed by U.S. to help Greece and Turkey resist the threats of communism

Twenty-One Demands –Japanese attempt to subjugate China in the Pre-WW I period

United Nations –world peace organization formed 1945

Vietnam War – (1964-1974) U.S. actively involved in containment of communist aggression; prior military advisement role (Eisenhower, Kennedy) escalated to full-scale combat by Johnson in '64; unpopularity of war at home led to withdrawal by Nixon in '74

Vietnamese "Boat People" – refugees who desperately sought to escape from communist takeover in 1970's by going to sea in flimsy vessels

Walensa, Lech – led Polish Solidarity Labor Movement; agitated for democratic reforms to end communist regime in Poland; elected President of free Poland in 1990

War Communism –Bolsheviks' command economic policy after U.S.S.R. was established, 1917-1919

Warlord – Chinese military dictators of each province after Republic founded in 1912

Warsaw Pact 1949 –alliance of Eastern European satellite nations; gave Soviet commanders control over the satellites' armies

World War I – (1914-1918)

World War II – (1939-45)

Yalta Conference – (1945) WW II Allied meeting; Roosevelt, Churchill, Stalin planned military and political arrangements to end war, and on formation of United Nations

Yeltsin, Boris – Russian Federation President; attempted to increase Gorbachev's reforms; held reform government together during the August 1991 coup in U.S.S.R.; presided over dissolution of the Soviet Union as Gorbachev resigned

Yom Kippur War –(1973) attack on Israel by Egypt & Syria on the Jewish Day of Atonement

Period Z   Due 8/2   P 117-18

Overpopulation, Hunger and Poverty

Barrios –overcrowded Latin American urban slums

Borlaug, Norman – Agronomist, a founder of the Green Revolution

Deforestation – over-cutting and waste of timber resources

Demographers – people who map population movements

Desertification – loss of available land to the desert

Ghettos –ethnic or cultural area or neighborhood

Green Revolution –program of scientific breakthroughs in agriculture used to help food production begun under U.N. supervision in 1960's

"Have Nots" – Third World countries; undeveloped nations

Humanitarianism – promotion of human welfare and social reform

Infrastructure –a society's total transport and communication system critical to development

International Monetary Fund (IMF) – U.N. financial agency aids less developed countries (LDC's)

Landed Aristocracy – traditional oligarchy exercising economic and indirect governing power through alliances with military juntas

Leached soil – minerals and nutrients washed away by constant rainfall

Monsoons –prevailing winds in East, South, and SE Asia; shift direction in summer and winter, cause uneven agricultural production

Nomadic – life-style of constant moving about, seeking food

Oasis –tiny fertile spot with water in desert

One-crop Economy – nearly all productive capacity of a nation or region tied to one cash crop; makes economy very susceptible to world demand; opposite of diversification.

Per Capita Income –total nat'l income ÷ population = share per person

Population Density – number of people per square mile

Subsistence Agriculture – producing barely for one's own needs

"Supercities" – concern over problems of unchecked urban growth

Third World – underdeveloped nations, unaligned in world politics

World Bank and IMF – International financial institutions to aid Third World nations finance capital projects

Economic Growth and Development

Age of Discovery – European exploration and colonization15th-16th C.

Agrarian – farm based life-style

Alliance for Progress – United States assistance policy for Latin America in 1960's

British Commonwealth of Nations – assoc. of former British colonies

Campesinos – paid laborers, tenant farmers, or peasants of Lat. America

Capitalist System –private enterprise (laissez-faire)

Cartel –combination of economic countries or companies to limit competition

Charter companies –private trading enterprises licensed by government; outposts became bases for colonies

Collective farms –large agricultural enterprises run by socialist gov't.

COMECON – former Council for Mutual Economic Assistance, 1949; Soviet-sponsored trade association for Eastern European satellites

Commercial Revolution – economic movement which opened Europe to world wide trade enterprises began in the 1400's

Common Market (EEC) – trade association of 12 Western European nations and 60 associate nations under the Lomé Convention

Communes – socialist cooperative farms

Creditor Nations – nations from whom others borrow money

Debtor Nations – nations owing large sums to others

Default –failure to make debt payments

Divesting – termination of investments in South Africa enterprises as an economic protest against apartheid policy

Domestic System –commercial production done in homes and coordinated by an entrepreneur

East India Company –Brit. trading co. set basis for colonial endeavors

Encomiendas – vast Latin American plantations; earlier, colonial land grants; Brazilian colonial land grants are "fazendas"

European Economic Community –see Common Market

European Atomic Energy Community (Euratom) –Post WW II cooperative nuclear research and development

Five Year Plans – Soviet and Chinese command economic structures

Feudalism – landholding-based lord/vassal economic-political-social system of medieval Europe and Japan

Fief – feudal land grant to vassal by an overlord; self-sufficient manor

Four Modernizations – Deng Xiaopong's revision of China's economy

Free Market Systems – economic structures which operate according to the relationship of supply and demand with minimal gov't. regulation

French Union (also French Community) –France retained ties with former colonies; similar to British Commonwealth

Glasnost –Gorbachev's policies sought to revitalize Soviet political atmosphere; triggered democratic movements in E. Europe

Good Neighbor Policy –Franklin Roosevelt's Latin American policy

Gosplan – Soviet Union's central economic decision-making agency for resource allocation and production goals

Gross National Product (GNP) – sum of the value of all goods and services produced in a country in a given in a year; helps measure economic health

"Have nots" – Third World countries; undeveloped nations

"Haves" – the developed, educated, wealthy, industrial nations

Industrial Revolution – socio-political change occurring when production of basic necessities becomes organized mechanically; began on large scale in England c. 1750

International Monetary Fund (IMF) – U.N. financial agency aids Third World development

Joint Stock Company –private enterprises used by English to finance exploration and colonization projects, 16th-19th C.

Kibbutz - system of Israeli collective farms

Landed Aristocracy – traditional oligarchy exercising economic and indirect governing power through alliances with military juntas

Lome Convention – wide-ranging 1975 economic trade agreement for 60 African and Asian nations with the European Common Market

8/2/93

Mercantilism –establishing colonies as government-sponsored private business enterprises to bring wealth to mother country

Mixed Economic System – combines elements of market and command

Multinational Corporations – major business enterprises in many nations: Unilever, Mitsubishi, ITT, GM, Exxon, Shell, Nestelé

Neo-Colonialism – a new form of political or economic control exercised by industrial states over underdeveloped nations

New Economic Policy (NEP; – (1919-1924) Lenin's socialist economic structure for the U.S.S.R.

Opportunity Cost –economic cost of making choices and trade-offs

Perestroika – Gorbachev's proposals for restructuring U.S.S.R.'s economy

Satellite Status – military, economic, and political domination of a country by an outside power (cf. neo-colonialism)

Scramble for Africa –European imperialistic competition in 19th C.

Silicon Chip – low-cost electronic computer technology

Ten Hours Act –1847 British law limited work for women, children

Trans-Siberian Railroad – opened U.S.S.R.'s Siberian region to development in 20th C.

Zaibatsu – large, powerful Japanese corporations

Environmental and Energy Concerns

Acid rain – air pollutants that travel in precipitation

Amazon River – massive basin in the center of South America, endangered by deforestation

Anoxia –oxygen depletion caused by air pollution

Chernobyl – 1986 nuclear power-plant accident in U.S.S.R.

Control of Pollution Act –British environmental regulations, 1974

Deforestation – over-cutting and waste of timber resources

Desertification – loss of available land to the desert

Environment – the physical settings in which people live

Greenhouse Effect – environmental pollution altering climatic patterns

Grid-lock –enormous traffic congestion bringing modern cities to a standstill

Leached soil – minerals & nutrients washed away by constant rainfall

OPEC –Organization of Petroleum Exporting Countries; oil cartel

Role Model Cities – present -day Zurich, Edinburgh, Leningrad, and Beijing demonstrate positive alternatives for desirable urban living

Toxic Waste –dangerous poisons, chemicals, and materials

Human Rights

Abolitionist movement – 19th C. anti-slavery movement in Western Europe & U.S.

African National Congress – ANC, South African civil rights group

Afrikaners – Boers; White decedents original Dutch colonists in South Africa; created apartheid system

Anti-Semitism –anti-Jewish feeling

Apartheid – South African government policy of total racial separation
Bill of Rights – limited power of monarchs in England, 1689
Dissidents –those who disagree with governmental policies
Groups Area Act – divided 13% of South Africa among 10 Bantu homelands, 1950
Gulag Archipelago –work critical of Soviet system by exiled dissident Aleksandr Solzhenitsyn officially censured 1968
Habeas Corpus Act – 17th C., guaranteed arrested Englishmen a statement of charges, bail, and a fair and speedy trial
Helsinki Accord of 1975 – human right agreements
Magna Carta – guarantee of rights signed in 1215 by English King John
Natural Rights of Man – basic human rights theories growing out of Enlightenment
Pass Laws –South African laws stated that all non-whites over 16 must carry passbooks which restricted where they could travel and work; repealed in 1984
Pasternak, Boris –Soviet writer: *Dr. Zhivago*; denied the right to accept the Nobel prize 1958; publication of the book in the Soviet Union was denied because it was critical of communism
Pogroms – violent purges, against Jews in Russia and Austrian Empires
Solzhenitsyn, Aleksandr – dissident author expelled from U.S.S.R. 1970's

Determination of Economic and Political Systems

Absolutism – concentration and exercise of ruling power usually by a monarch
Age of Imperialism – 19th C. African and Asian colonization by European industrial nations for raw materials
Anti-imperialism – strong desire for freedom from foreign control
Arab Nationalism –movement to unify Arab nations
Arab Socialism –improvement of socio-economic conditions for all Arabs
Aristocracy –government by a small, privileged class
Ashikaga Shogunate –feudal Japanese rulers, 1338-1567
Bicameral – two-house legislative body: British Parliament, Japanese Diet, U.S. Congress
Byzantine Empire – Eastern Roman Empire reached its peak in 4th and 5th C. A.D.
Cabinet of Ministers – power group in contemporary Japanese gov't.
Caliph – title for successor to Mohammed as spiritual leader of Islam
Cape-to-Cairo Railroad – Cecil Rhodes project for linking British territories along Africa's east coast
Capitalist system –private enterprise, with minimum government regulation (laissez-faire)
Cartel –combination of economic units to limit competition
Caudillo – local ruler with dictatorial power in Latin America
Central American Federation – post-independence attempt at unification, c. 1820
Chauvinism – nationalist extremism in 19th & 20th C. Germany
Chin (Qin) Dynasty – unified China 221 B. C. - 210 B.C.

City-states –Sparta and Athens ancient Greece

Codified Laws –organized and written legal system

Committee of Public Safety - operated the Reign of Terror during the French Revolution which resulted in the execution of 15-45,000 opponents in the 1790's

Communist Manifesto – Karl Marx's work: extreme socialist doctrine

Communist Party – General Secretary is powerful position in U.S.S.R.

Confucianism – basic socio-political philosophy of China - ancient times

Congress of the People's Deputies – Soviet Union's new elected body that chooses the President and the Supreme Soviet

Constantinople – central city of E. Roman Empire; formerly Byzantium

Constitutional Monarchy –Britain's system of limited monarchy and Parliamentary rule

Cultural Revolution – mid-60's internal power struggle in Maoist China

Declaration of Independence –U.S. revolutionary document by Thomas Jefferson reflected Enlightenment ideas of Locke, Rousseau

Democratic Socialism –mixed economic systems in European nations with extensive welfare systems

Dictatorship of the Proletariat – Marxist dogma that indicates working classes will eventually rule society for the benefit of all

Diet – two-house national legislature of Japan

Direct Democracy –citizens having direct say in the making of decisions rather than being represented by officials

Divine Right –claim that absolute power comes from God

Dollar Diplomacy – interventions U.S.- Latin American Policy of early 20th C. based on protection of commercial investment

Duma –Russian national legislative body under Tsars in 19th & 20th C.

Emancipation Act in 1861 – Tsar Alexander II freed Russian serfs

Embargo – refusal to sell to or trade with other nations

Enlightened Despot – ruler who uses autocratic power for the benefit of the people

Enlightenment –intellectual movement in 17th and 18th centuries began a search for natural laws that governed man's existence; Locke, Voltaire, Montesquieu, Smith, Paine

Estates General – French Parliament, c. 18th C.

Factory Act – (1833) protection for British workers

Four Modernizations – Deng Xiaopong's revision of China's economy

Free Market Systems – economic structures which operate according to the relationship of supply and consumer demand with minimal government regulation

Fuehrer – German title for leader used by Hitler

Fujiwara Family – ruled Japan 10th –12th C. A.D.

Good Neighbor Policy –F. D. Roosevelt's Lat. American policy, c. 1933

Gosplan – Soviet Union's central economic decision-making agency for resource allocation and production goals

Glorious Revolution – England'sCatholic James II deposed; replaced by Protestant William & Mary, 1688

Government of India Act – British began structure for home rule, 1935

Gran Colombia – short-lived union of Venezuela, Columbia, Peru, Ecuador, and Bolivia, c. 1820

Great Depression –worldwide economic collapse 1929-1940; social and political upheaval in Germany laid groundwork for Nazi movement

Great Leap Forward – Mao's massive economic reorganization in China which largely failed, 1950's

Great Reform Bill –19th C.; British reform which gave middle classes the right to vote

Gross National Product (GNP) – sum of the value of all goods and services produced in a country in a given in a year; helps measure economic health

Han Dynasty – (210 B.C. - 220 A.D.) expanded China's control in Asia

Hierarchy – ascending order of leaders

Hungarian Revolution – democratic reform attempt harshly suppressed by Soviet Army in 1956

"Have nots" – Third World countries; undeveloped nations

"Haves" – the developed, educated, wealthy, industrial nations

Inflation –period of significantly rising prices without a counterbalancing rise in production; demand outweighs supply, causing prices to rise

Instrument of Government – England under Cromwell's Puritan rule in the 1650's, first modern written constitution

Junta – committee of military rulers

Justinian Code – 6th C. A.D. collection of civil law, preserving Roman legal heritage; has had great impact on the concept of human rights

Irish Free State – Eire; independence from England achieved in WW I

Khmer Rouge – communist insurgents in Cambodian civil war, 1960-80

Manchu-Ching – Chinese dynasty, 1644 - 1912

Mandate – right or command

Marx, Karl – 19th century author *Communist Manifesto, Das Kapital*

Marxism – Economic interpretation of history, Class struggle, Surplus Value Theory, and the Inevitability of Socialism

Meiji Restoration –industrial era reorgan. of Japan's power structure

Model Parliament – English legislative prototype, 1295 A.D.; established the concept of the "power of the purse" (Parliamentary control of national finances)

Morley-Minto Reforms –Parliament broadened Indians' participation in colonial government, 1908-09

National Congress Party –Indian ruling party 1948-89; lost control, 1989

National Convention –power group in French Revolution, led by Robespierre, Danton, and Marat

National Socialist German Workers Party –Nazi Party; in control 1933-45

Nepotism – appointing family members to key positions in government

Oligarchy –control of decision making by a small group

Ottoman Empire – major Muslim political structure, 14th-20th C.

Parliament – British legislative body holds chief decision making power

Peninsularies –Iberian-born nobles; crown appointed rulers in colonial Latin America

Petition of Right –1628 act strengthened British Parliament's power

Precedents –past actions and decisions that act as traditional models

Prime Minister –the nation's chief executive; British Prime Minister is the majority leader of the House of Commons

Puritan Revolution –(1642) overthrow of British monarchy

Quotations of Chairman Mao –book of Mao's communist philosophy

Reichstag –lower house of the German parliament where Hitler captured power in 1933

Republic of China – (Taiwan gov't. in exile) Kuomintang forces retreated to Taiwan after defeat by communists in 1949 on mainland China.

Restoration Period –rule of Charles II in 1660's after the English Puritan Revolution

Russification –imperialist policy in which conquered people were forced to adopt the Russian language, culture and religion in an attempt to increase the degree of unity within the country

Salt March – Gandhi's non-violent protest of British tax system

Serfs –feudal peasants legally bound to the land

Socialism – system in which the means of production are controlled by the state to varying degrees

Sparta – ancient Greek city-state, ruled as military oligarchy

Spheres of Influence –imperialistic sectioning off of China trade by European powers in late 19th and early 20th C.

Sultan –title used by Arabian imperial rulers

Superpowers – powerful political states (U.S. and U.S.S.R.)

Supreme Soviet – Soviet Union's national legislative body

Taiwan (Republic of China) – S. China Sea island stronghold of anticommunist gov't-in-exile established by Chinese nationalists c. 1945

Three Principles of the People – basic political philosophy of Chinese Republic's founder, Sun Yat-sen, c. 1912

Tokugawa Shogunate – powerful feudal rulers of Japan, 1603-1868; Seclusion Policy – diplomatic isolation of Japan, 17th-19th C. A.D.

Totalitarian Government - absolutist government exercising total control over all aspects of the lives of the people

Tributary system –Chinese dynasties required conquered regions to send tribute [gifts] to the Manchu overlords

Tsar – Russian Emperor; also spelled as czar and tzar

Tudors – English dynasty, 1485-1603 Turks Middle East ruling group 1450-1915 A.D.; see Ottoman Empire

Twelve Tables –codified laws of the ancient Romans

Union of South Africa – unified Cape Colony, Transvaal, and Orange Free State into semi-autonomous state in British Empire c. 1910; became independent Republic of South Africa in 1961

Vassals – knights swearing oaths of loyalty to the more powerful nobles in Medieval European feudal system

Viceroys –authoritarian crown governors of Spain's Latin American colonial regions: New Spain, Peru, New Grenada, and LaPlata

Weimar Republic – weak German government, 1919-33; laid groundwork Westernization – Peter the Great's attempts to emulate Europe and modernize 17th C. Russian society

Yamato Clan Leaders –first emperors of Japan, c. 220 A.D.

Yoritomo –first military ruler to take the title Shogun, 1155 A.D.

Zionism –Herzl founded movement for a Jewish homeland in 1897

Historic and Contemporary Political Figures by Region

Africa

Kenyatta, Jomo –nationalist leader; 1st President of Kenya

Leopold, King of Belgium – established Belgian Congo colony in central Africa, began the imperialist "Scramble for Africa", c. 1880's

Mandela, Nelson –South African anti-apartheid leader

Nkrumah, Kwame – nationalist leader and first President of Ghana

Nyerere, Julius – nationalist leader and first President of Tanzania

Rhodes, Cecil –Brit. imperialist built colonial empire in S. and E. Africa, 19th C.

Tutu, Bishop Desmond – South African anti-apartheid leader; awarded 1984 Nobel Peace Prize

South and Southeast Asia

Aquino, Corazon –deposed Marcos regime; Pres. of Philippines, 1986

Bhutto, Benazir – Pakistan's first woman President (1986–1990)

Clive, Sir Robert - military leader laid basis for British rule in India

Gandhi, Indira – daughter of Nehru; Indian Prime Minister, 1966-84; assassinated by Siks

Gandhi, Mohandas –non-violent Indian independence movement leader, assassinated 1948

Gandhi, Rajiv – Indian Prime Minister, 1984-1989; assassinated 1991

Ho Chi Minh –communist guerrilla leader, Pres. of N. Vietnam; d. 1969

Marcos, Ferdinand – Philippines dictator, 1965-86; deposed by Corazon Aquino; d.1989

Mohammed Ali Jinnah – founder Muslim state of Pakistan, 1947

Nehru, Jawaharlal –disciple of Gandhi in the Congress Party, became the first Prime Minister, 1948-1964

East Asia

Chiang Kai-shek – military leader of Chinese Nationalist government & the Kuomintang party

Deng Xiaopong – reformist Chinese leader after Mao, '76- , ordered repression of student democracy demonstrations in 1989

Heng Samrin – Kampuchean leader 1980- ; former Khmer Rouge leader

Khan, Ghengis – 13th c. A.D. Mongol conqueror

Jiang Zemin – General Secretary of Chinese Communist Party, replaced Zhao after Ti'ananmen Square Massacre in 1989

Li Peng – Chinese Premier who unleashed troops in brutal repression of the Chinese students demonstrating for democracy in Beijing's Ti'ananman Square in 1989

Mao Zedong – Chinese leader, est. communist regime, 1949; d.1976

Zhao Ziyang –former Premier and General Secretary of the Communist Party of People's Republic of China; sided with students in 1989 Beijing Democracy Demonstrations

Latin America

Bolivar, Simon – revolutionary liberator of Columbia, Venezuela c. 1820

Castro, Fidel –Cuban communist leader, 1959-

Columbus, Christopher – explorer in pay of Spanish Crown credited with beginning the Age of Colonization in Latin America

Jose de San Martin – 19th C. South American liberator

Juarez, Benito –revered Mexican reformer of 1850's

L'Overture, Toussaint - self-educated black slave, led insurrection in 1791 against the French & established the Dominican Republic

O'Higgins, Bernardo –South American nationalist leader, liberator of Chile, c. 1810-1823

Ortega, Daniel –Nicaraguan communist leader (1980–1990)

Peron, Juan – Argentine dictator; d. 1974

Pinochet, Augosto Ugarte - repressive military junta, Chilean Pres., 1973-

Middle East

Alexander the Great – Hellenistic conqueror & unifier of ancient Middle East; d. 323 B.C.

Arafat, Yassir – leader of Palestine Liberation Organization

Ataturk, Mustapha Kemel –Turkish WW I hero, established the Republic of Turkey in 1923

Herzl, Theodor – 19th C. founder Zionist Movement - Jewish homeland

Khomeini, Ruhollah – leader of Iranian Shi'ite Muslims who over threw Shah in 1978; d.1989

Nasser, Gamal Abdul – nationalist leader of Egypt in 1950's

Pahlavi, Shah Muhammed Reza –ruler of Iran, 1952-78; overthrown by Shi'ite fundamentalist movement in 1978 Iranian Revolution

Sadat, Anwar – Egyptian President signed Camp David Accords with Israel; assassinated 1981

Sulieman the Magnificent –ruled over golden age of Ottoman Empire, 1520-1566

Western Europe

Bismarck, Otto von – German chancellor responsible for forging Prussia into modern-day Germany, and building it into a major military and commercial power; d. 1898

Bonaparte, Napoleon – French General , led 1795 coup; later crowned himself Emperor of the French; extensive military conquests; defeated and exiled in 1815 by Holy Alliance

Caesar Augustus – first Roman Emperor, c. 27 B.C.

Caesar, Julius – military dictator of Rome, d. 44 B.C.

Charlemagne –8th C. A.D. leader of Franks; formed Holy Roman Empire

Charles I –British king, dethroned & beheaded in Puritan Revolution, mid-1600's

Charles II –British king, restored to monarchy after Cromwell's death in 1658

Churchill, Winston S. – charismatic WW II Prime Minister of Britain, helped shape post war world at summits; warned of Soviet power in famous "Iron Curtain" speech; d.1965

Colbert – mercantilist finance minister and advisor to France's absolutist King Louis XIV

Constantine the Great – Roman Emperor; Edict of Milan, 313 A.D.

Cromwell, Oliver –British Puritan dictator, declared Lord Protector 1653-1658

Elizabeth I – near-absolute monarch of England in 16th C., established the nation as a power in Europe

Gladstone, William –19th C. British Prime Minister; imperialism

Henry VIII –Tudor king of England, created Anglican church

Hitler, Adolf – fascist leader of Nazi Germany, 1933-45

Isabella, Queen of Spain –financed the voyage of Columbus, 1492

James II –English king deposed in Glorious Revolution, 1688

Kaiser Wilhelm II –German monarch, c. WW I

Louis XIV – (1643-1715)French monarch absolute power ("Sun King"- monarch as center of all existence); rebuilt France into major military and commercial power with overseas empire.

Mazzini –nationalist organizer helped unify Italy, 19th C.

Mussolini, Benito – Italian Fascist leader, 1922-40's

Philip II of Spain –armada defeated by naval forces of Elizabeth I of England in famous English Channel battle 1588

Pope Urban II – called for a crusade to regain control of the Holy Land from the Muslim Turks in 1095 A.D.

Thatcher, Margaret –conservative British Prime Minister, first woman to hold position; (1979–1990)

William III (of Orange) and **Mary II** – 17th C. English monarchs installed after Glorious Revolution, after Stuart King James II was deposed

Eastern Europe, Russia, and Central Asia

Alexander I –Russian Tsar, stopped Napoleonic advance; d. 1825

Alexander II –Russian Tsar; abolished serfdom, est. Duma; d.1881

Brezhnev, Leonid –U.S.S.R. leader, 1965–1983

Catherine the Great –absolutist Russian Tsarina, 1762-1796

Ceausescu, Nicolae –Ruthless Romanian communist leader, in power 1967, overthrown and executed 1989 by general reform movement

Dubcek, Alexander – democratic reformer of Czechoslovakian Communist Party, ousted by 1968 invasion by U.S.S.R. and E. European satellites; Speaker of new Parliament after 1989 reform movement

Gorbachev, Mikhail – Soviet reform leader; negotiated end to Cold War; ended Soviet dominance of Eastern Europe; began *glasnost* democratic constitutional reforms and *peristroika* economic reforms; became Soviet leader in 1984, elected President in 1989, and resigned Soviet Presidency with the collapse of the U.S.S.R. in 1991

Ivan III (Ivan the Great) –1462-1505; overthrew Tartars in 1480

Ivan IV (Ivan the Terrible) – absolutist Russian ruler, 1533-1584

Khrushchev, Nikita S. – Soviet leader 1956-65; escalated Cold War tensions, space race

Lenin, Vladimir Ilyich –Marxist leader of Boshevks in 1917 Russian Revolution; became first leader of the U.S.S.R.

Nicholas I – repressive Russian Tsar, 1825-1855

Nicholas II – Tsar deposed by 1917 Revolutions, assassinated, 1917

Peter the Great – Tsar, 1682-1725, attempted to westernize Russian culture and economy

Romanov, Michael – founded the Romanov dynasty in 1615 which ruled Russia until the Bolshevik Revolution in 1917

Stalin, Josef –autocratic Soviet dictator, 1925-53

Walensa, Lech – led Polish Solidarity Labor Movement; agitated for democratic reforms to end communist regime in Poland; elected President of free Poland in 1990

Yeltsin, Boris – Russian Federation President; attempted to increase Gorbachev's reforms; held reform government together during the August 1991 coup in U.S.S.R.; presided over dissolution of the Soviet Union as Gorbachev resigned

Religious Terms

Allah – Muslim name for God

Ancestor Worship –in African and Asian religions, forebearers are considered a living part of the spiritual community

Anglican Church –made state religion of England by Henry VIII, Act of Supremacy , 1534

Animism – belief that objects contain a spirit

Bible – sacred scriptures of Judeo-Christian religion

Brahma – Hindu Deity, the creator

Buddhism – major religion of eastern and central Asia

Buddha – the Enlightened One, founder of Buddhism, 6th C. B.C.

Calvin, John - Swiss theologian, leader of European Protestant Reformation, c. 1560 A.D.

Castes – rigid Hindu system of hereditary social groupings dictating one's rank and occupation

Catholic Counter-Reformation – church reform movement in the 16th C. to offset effects of Protestant Reformation

Christianity – Major world religion based on teachings of Jesus Christ; Old & New Testaments of the Bible; Judaic ethics; includes Roman Catholic, Protestant, Eastern Orthodox and Coptic Rites

Council of Trent – 16th C. reorganization of the Catholic Church in response to the Protestant Reformation

Dharma – sacred duty one owes to family and caste

Ecumenism – movement to seek unity among different religions

Edict of Milan – granted freedom of worship to all Christians in Roman Empire, 313 A.D.

Eightfold Path – Buddhism's basic religious concepts

Excommunication –depriving a person of church membership

Five Pillars – basic beliefs and duties of Muslim faith

Four Noble Truths – basic beliefs of Buddhism

Gautama, Siddarta –founder of Buddhist faith, 6th C. B.C.

Hinduism – major religion of India
Holy Land – Israel/Palestine
Huguenots – French Protestant group, Calvinists
Islam – world religion founded in Middle East by prophet Mohammed, 7th C.
   A.D.; includes Sunni and Shi'ite sects focus of Muslim culture
Jesus Christ – founder Christianity; major world religion
John Paul II –Roman Catholic Pope; (1978)
Judaism – major world religion; c.1400 B.C.; belief in one God, social justice,
   and moral law
Judeo-Christian Ethic – primary shaper of the values, ideals, and cultures
   of the western world
Karma –idea that a person's actions carry unavoidable consequences and
   determine the nature of subsequent reincarnation
Koran – Islam's sacred text
Luther, Martin – German cleric credited with beginning the Protestant
   Reformation, c. 1517
Mecca –Islamic holy city, Saudi Arabia
Mohammed – originator and major prophet of Islamic faith, 570-632A.D.
Monotheism – belief in a single of deity
Mosque –a house of worship for Muslims
Moses –law-giver, leader of ancient Hebrew civilization
New Testament –the Christian Gospels of Evangelists Matthew, Mark,
   Luke, and John
Nirvana – Hindu cycle of reincarnation broken when one achieves a perfect
   state of mind
Old Testament –Bible; holy scripture contained the teachings and law
   required for the moral behavior of the Jews and Christians
Polytheism – belief in a multiplicity of gods
Protestant Reformation – break in the Christian Church c. 1517; led by
   Calvin, Knox, Luther,Zwingli; caused realignment of political power, and
   religious wars for more than a century.
Puritans –Calvinist reformers of Anglicanism; c. 1600's
Rabbis –Jewish religious teachers
Reincarnation – Hindu belief in rebirth of the soul in another form of life
Schism – intense disagreement leads to split usually in religious sect
Shari'a –Islamic moral rules are incorporated into a code of law
Shintoism –Japanese religion; worships nature and ancestors; some
   blending with Buddhism
Sikhs –militant Hindu sect founded in the 15th century; history of resisting
   Indian government
Talmud – holy book of Judaic faith, knowledge, and ethics
Vatican (City) – sovereign state inside Rome, Italy; center of Roman
   Catholic Church; residence of popes
Taoism –ancient Chinese philosophy; revered nature, self-knowledge,
   simplicity
Theocracy –government ruled by religious officials
Torah –Hebrew holy scripture; books of the Old Testament
Zen Buddhism – popular among Japanese samurai; required meditation
   called for much self-discipline